Having discovered Christ at an early age in a church that believes in and practices the supernatural, Iris Delgado writes out of her own experiences. She writes with clarity and candor regarding the need of the miraculous in the life of each believer. She shows the reader how to experience personal miracles. I believe the miracle-working power of God will be released in your life as you read this practical account of how miracles are received.

—PASTOR J. DON GEORGE
FOUNDING PASTOR, CALVARY CHURCH, IRVING, TEXAS
CALVARYCHURCH.CC

Dr. Iris Delgado, writing under the inspiration of the Holy Spirit, once again reveals her God-given ability to bridge the natural to the supernatural. The reality of miracles today is a difficult concept for many. The scriptural foundation linked with Iris's personal experience leaves the reader with a deep assurance that "in God all things are possible." I heartily endorse this new book, *Satan, You Can't Have My Miracle*.

—DR. RONALD E. SHORT
APOSTLE AND TEACHER
RONALD E. SHORT EVANGELISTIC ASSOCIATION
IDABEL, OK

In the midst of these turbulent times God has anointed Dr. Iris Delgado to write in an extraordinary way that will inspire, equip, and, most importantly, impart principles to receive personal healing and miracles through divine inspiration. The book is a must-read for all people who desire to walk in the supernatural realm of the Holy Spirit in everyday life.

—DR. RAUL LOPEZ JR.
SENIOR PASTOR, MAXIMUM PRAISE HOUSE OF WORSHIP
VEGA BAJA, PUERTO RICO
MAXIMAALABANZA.ORG

Dr. Iris Delgado lives the words that she has penned in this literary work. This book about the supernatural power of God is not only theory; she has walked out every sentence with a life dedicated to Jesus Christ. Open your heart and embrace her expounding on God's proven Word of truth. Dr. Delgado will let you know that God is never the problem—He is our *only* answer.

—Dr. Duane & Darilyn Bemis
For God's Glory Ministries
Big Spring, Texas
Fggbemis.org

SATAN, YOU CAN'T HAVE MY MIRACLE

IRIS DELGADO

CHARISMA
HOUSE

Most CHARISMA HOUSE BOOK GROUP products are available at special quantity discounts for bulk purchase for sales promotions, premiums, fundraising, and educational needs. For details, write Charisma House Book Group, 600 Rinehart Road, Lake Mary, Florida 32746, or telephone (407) 333-0600.

SATAN, YOU CAN'T HAVE MY MIRACLE by Iris Delgado
Published by Charisma House
Charisma Media/Charisma House Book Group
600 Rinehart Road
Lake Mary, Florida 32746
www.charismahouse.com

Unless otherwise noted, all Scripture quotations are from the New King James Version of the Bible. Copyright © 1979, 1980, 1982 by Thomas Nelson, Inc., publishers. Used by permission.

Scripture quotations marked AMP are from the Amplified Bible. Old Testament copyright © 1965, 1987 by the Zondervan Corporation. The Amplified New Testament copyright © 1954, 1958, 1987 by the Lockman Foundation. Used by permission.

Scripture quotations marked KJV are from the King James Version of the Bible.

Scripture quotations marked NAS are from the New American Standard Bible, copyright © 1960, 1962, 1963, 1968, 1971, 1972, 1973, 1975, 1977, 1995 by The Lockman Foundation. Used by permission. (www.Lockman .org)

Scripture quotations marked NLT are from the Holy Bible, New Living Translation, copyright © 1996, 2004, 2007. Used by permission of Tyndale House Publishers, Inc., Wheaton, IL 60189. All rights reserved.

Scripture quotations marked The Message are from The Message: The Bible in Contemporary English, copyright © 1993, 1994, 1995, 1996, 2000, 2001, 2002. Used by permission of NavPress Publishing Group.

Cover design by Justin Evans
Design Director: Bill Johnson

Visit the author's website at www.crownedwithpurpose.com.

Library of Congress Cataloging-in-Publication Data:
Delgado, Iris.
  Satan, you can't have my miracle / Iris Delgado. -- 1st ed.
      p. cm.
  Includes bibliographical references.
  ISBN 978-1-61638-878-2 (trade paper) -- ISBN 978-1-61638-879-9
(e-book)
  1. Miracles. 2. Spiritual healing. 3. Spiritual warfare. I. Title.
  BT97.3.D45 2012
  231.7'3--dc23

                              2012028031

While the author has made every effort to provide accurate telephone numbers and Internet addresses at the time of publication, neither the publisher nor the author assumes any responsibility for errors or for changes that occur after publication.

First edition

12 13 14 15 16 — 987654321
Printed in the United States of America

DEDICATION

I DEDICATE THIS BOOK to all the people who need a miracle. It may be that you need a miracle from an incurable and devastating disease, the salvation of someone you dearly love, or divine intervention of something only God can make possible. Perhaps you desperately need a miraculous inner healing from recurring trauma from your past or from something going on right now.

I also dedicate this book to the millions of sick and wounded men, women, and young people who have experienced some kind of physical or mental abuse or an enslaving addiction, and you are still trying to cope and deal with the effects and present circumstances or the lingering memories.

Some of you may have a serious illness caused by the trauma and stress of hardships and adversities from your past and present relationships. Some of you may be living with a confused identity, trapped in your own body.

God is no respecter of persons. The miraculous things that God did through Jesus Christ His Son during His time on earth He will also do for you. I am a recipient of God's miraculous power at work today and a witness to many miracles and healings that have truly made a believer out of me.

To you who need a miracle or a healing, I pray that the Holy Spirit will reveal truth to you as you read the pages of this book and that you too will be a recipient of God's miraculous love and healing power.

CONTENTS

SUPERNATURAL MIRACLES AND HEALING

IS GOD STILL DOING THIS TODAY?

HAVE YOU BEEN asking God for a miracle of healing, and instead things seem to be getting worse? Have you been experiencing frustration and anxiety because you have done everything the Word says you should do, but you still can't see a glimmer of hope in your situation? Have you been battling with inner turmoil, and everything you do seems to end up in failure?

Writing this book has been a tremendous challenge. The devil doesn't want the message of miracles, supernatural divine healing, and soul restoration to get out. My intent is to be precise, biblically correct, and, at the same time, convey the truth that miracles, healing, and restoration from all kinds of strongholds are available and obtainable today to all who dare to believe in Jesus Christ, the Messiah.

I myself have experienced many miracles, some of healing from a debilitating and incurable illness, some of protection from impending accidents and armed robbery, and some of healing from abuse and hatred.

Throughout these pages I want to expose the lies of Satan that have blinded many people into thinking that miracles are only for some people. I also want to build up your faith through the real testimonies of healing and miracles that I have personally witnessed. You will gain specific tools that will help you believe God for the impossible. You will learn how to pray and confess God's Word for your situation, how to use your weapons of spiritual warfare, and how to set yourself or someone else free from any kind of bondage or torment from the past.

The information in this book is meant to prepare you to believe and receive miraculous divine intervention and healing from all demonic strongholds. To fully know God, we must know Him as the healer. "For I am the LORD who heals you" (Exod. 15:26).

CHAPTER ONE

THE MIRACLE OF SOUL TRANSFORMATION

*He sent His word and healed them, and delivered
them from their destructions.*

—PSALM 107:20

I FOUND HER ON her bed curled up in a fetus position. Her young body heaved back and forth without consolation. Tears rolled down her cheeks into a pillow now soiled with mascara, drenched with the agony of a soul suffering in silence. My unexpected presence startled this young woman who painfully sat up, unable to answer my astonished question, "What's wrong?" As I gently enveloped her in my arms, I felt her body throbbing as a surge of anguished desperation exhaled and unleashed from the depth of her being.

This precious young woman, my firstborn daughter, had been suffering in silence for much of the two years of her troubled marriage. After the divorce it took a long time to repair the damage inflicted to her soul. God in His mercy kept her from succumbing to a life of uncertainty and misery. I do believe that my constant prayers for my children have been effective and powerful. She went through a spiritual process of inner healing. Today, years later, my daughter is strong, self-confident, and unhindered to enjoy God's promises for her life. Without the miracle of divine intervention where the Holy Spirit and man participate together, my daughter could have become an insecure, unhappy, and unfulfilled young woman, tormented by evil spirits.

From Oppression to Freedom

Not all couples who go through divorce heal easily. Not all people who have been abused get over it quickly. Not all people who go through bankruptcy recover. Many people go through tragic experiences, and some through agonizing sickness, unable to live a fulfilling life. This section is about the miracle of healing and transformation of the soul—the part of us that cries out silently and wonders, "How can I become free?" Perhaps you may be one of the few who never feel oppression from the enemy, but you may know someone who is desperate to experience freedom. I pray that the Holy Spirit will help us understand the urgency and tremendous need for teaching and awareness of what the enemy is really up to and the things we can do to become whole again. God wants us to enjoy all the blessings of the new covenant.

- Do you feel as if life is passing you by and doubt that it will get any better?
- How can an emotionally depressed, brokenhearted, and abused person get healed?
- Can a person really be set free from tormenting evil spirits?
- What kind of power is this, and how can a person activate this power?
- Do all believers have power and authority over all the power of the enemy?
- What about the victims? Once they accept Christ, can they also depend on God's authority and power to receive healing and restoration?
- What about curses transferred from one family member to another? Can they be broken and the person set free?
- What about messing with the occult? Will that really affect a person's life and character in any way?

I believe that once a person is born again and receives knowledge of his new covenant rights in Christ Jesus, he can answer *yes* to all of these questions. The Bible clearly reveals to us that all citizens of the kingdom of heaven have been given supernatural authority over all the wicked power of the enemy: "Behold, I give you the authority to trample on serpents and scorpions, and over all the power of the enemy, and nothing shall by any means hurt you" (Luke 10:19). But the problem is that too many Christians do not know how to get free from hindering habits or situations they have been placed in through someone else. They have no idea how to use their kingdom authority.

This generation has produced a great number of adults, children, and young people who are totally unhappy, battling with emotional disorders and unfulfilled dreams. Many adults will try to put the blame on others, but I firmly believe this generation is being molded by parents who are too busy to notice what's taking place around them, by an educational system that has taken God and prayer out of their atmosphere, and by a world system intent on instant self-gratification. Through TV programs, media entertainment, games, schoolbooks, technology, and friendships we are constantly being fed secular and New Age beliefs and a lifestyle defying all the laws of the new covenant established by God for man to succeed and multiply.

If that weren't enough, this week as I write, Satan has been actively influencing people and children to kill and abuse. CNN News reported that a Los Angeles–area school was at the center of a shocking child abuse scandal after the discovery of two teachers abusing innocent children.[1] Many of these children, undoubtedly, will grow up with traumatic memories, and some may develop irrational behaviors. It is situations such as these that cause ingrained abnormal behaviors in children, who then become adults needing divine intervention and transformation.

Then I heard in the news the bizarre details of a dad burning down his house, killing himself and his two sons, after the search for his missing wife.[2] This was a young dad with a lovely young family and a full life ahead of him but with a messed-up mind and soul, dabbling in child porn and exposing himself to the pounding attacks of the enemy. Every area of our society is being affected by sin and the attacks of the enemy.

The number of terminal patients is rising, and many are being sent home because all avenues of medical and psychiatric help have been exhausted. Just like in the times of Jesus's ministry on earth, millions of desperate people are waiting for a powerful anointing that will heal the sick and break the yokes of bondage. Today we need to hear the words and commands of Jesus coming out of God's people, breaking through the crowds, commanding evil spirits to loose the people, sickness and disease to let go their grip, blind eyes and deaf ears to be opened, death to give up its young and suicidal victims, and the curse of poverty to release the people. God is waiting for us to take up our authority over all the power of the enemy, which He has already delegated to all born-again believers (Luke 10:19).

I believe that miracles, signs, and wonders are available to us every day, just as our daily bread is provided to us by God's divine intervention each day, but there's a commitment we must make. I like the way Jennifer LeClaire, news editor at *Charisma*, puts it in one of her newsletters:

> We can't do the Lord's part—we can't force miracles, signs and wonders. But we can do our part—we can tear down the strongholds in our own souls that are preventing us from walking in the fullness of the Spirit. We can stop tolerating spirits that tempt us to sin. We can start interceding for the fallen saints instead of playing judge. In other words, we can start living like the saints lived in the book of Acts: sold out, on fire and ready to die for the gospel. Revival begins with you.
>
> Again, we can't manufacture miracles. We can't work up wonders. But we can cooperate with the Holy Spirit to separate the profane from the holy in our own hearts and in

our own minds. We can purge ourselves and lay aside every weight that holds us back. We can allow the Spirit of God to do a deep work in us and so the Spirit of God can do a great work through us. Revival begins with you—and me.[3]

Today we are witnessing an unprecedented growth in many churches filling up with new converts, eagerly anticipating the anointing and power of God to be manifested after hearing messages of the miraculous power of God to heal and set a person free from poverty and from the power of Satan. What happens then? Where are the altar calls? Where are the anointed altar workers, ready to cast out demons and command sickness, disease, and brokenness to release the sick and burdened desperate people? Instead the music starts up again, announcements need to be made, and the people are told that the altars are open for prayer after the service is dismissed.

Where is the power of God to set the captives free? There are many Spirit-filled churches teaching the people how to be set free. But too many are seeker-friendly congregations with wonderful messages but no signs, wonders, and miracles following the Word of God. People come out feeling refreshed but with the same aggravating problems and hindrances. We are missing the most important part of the gospel: to heal the sick, open blind eyes, and bring out the prisoners from darkness and spiritual oppression (Isa. 42:7). God has already made provision by giving us a Savior, Jesus Christ.

The enemy is working overtime. He knows his time is short, because God is aligning everything to welcome His bride into the kingdom of heaven. God's people are the bride of Christ, and we must cleanse and prepare ourselves for this magnificent event. Too many people are hurting today. Every family has been affected by the unstable and debt-burdened economy; the loss of jobs, homes, retirement pensions, and health insurance; and the rise in divorce and broken homes. All this instability is causing desperation and high-level strife in many homes.

Children are hiding in their cyber world, and many are experiencing anxiety disorders.

We have never seen a time such as this one. Our world, as we know it, will soon cease to exist. A one-world system is quickly unfolding, and a socialist society is already in the making. God's people need to educate themselves and believe that God has a greater plan—and that He also has the last word! The just shall live by faith. We must commit our lives to live a holy life and believe that God is actively looking after us. We shall not fail, succumb, starve, or do without. God has promised to keep us and sustain us all the days of our lives. We must believe this.

We need a fresh vision.

The church today needs a fresh vision of what the Holy Spirit has always desired to do through His people. We cannot continue being independent of God's Spirit, doing ministry by the arm of the flesh. We need to have a total dependence on the Holy Spirit if we want to see radical manifestations of healing and miraculous deliverances.

I love the way F. F. Bosworth explains this topic in his book *Christ the Healer*, first published in 1924:

> The age in which we live was intended by our heavenly Father to be the most miraculous of all the dispensations. It is the Miracle-Worker's age; the Holy Spirit's dispensation. During this age the great promise is that God will pour out the Holy Spirit, the Miracle-Worker, upon all flesh. This is the only age in which the Miracle-Worker would incarnate Himself in us. This is the only age in which the nine gifts of the Spirit, including the gifts of faith, healing and miracles, were to be distributed to every man severally as He, the Holy Spirit, will. Jesus declared that the works that He was doing would be continued and that even "greater works" would be done by the Holy Spirit, the Miracle-Worker.

This was after He entered office during Christ's exaltation.
This is the Spirit's dispensation.[4]

Wow! I love this confirmation.

The things you read in this book are intended to bring common sense, understanding, and divine healing, especially for people who are going through trials and tribulations. It is not intended as a profound theological discourse or intellectual dissertation. My desire is to teach the ABCs of the miraculous power of God to heal, resident in all believers in Christ Jesus. This is phenomenal truth and information that so many people of this generation are missing or misunderstanding. Yes, I realize there is much information available on this subject, but this presentation is easy to understand and a how-to for you to put into practice. These principles will change your life forever if you apprehend them and take this counsel seriously.

There's a stirring and restlessness going on in the spirit realm. God is calling His ministers into accountability. We are beginning to see a hunger and a thirst among our young people everywhere for truth and transparency. They are tired of hypocrisy, because every time they put their eyes on a Christian hero, he may be the one falling into temptation and devastating his family and followers. God's mercy is extended to hurting people right now. We must take advantage of this window of opportunity and take immediate action to restore what the enemy has stolen.

What does this all have to do with the miraculous? Everything! God waits patiently to pour out His love and healing balm and to restore broken and hurting people. Without healing and transformation of the spirit, soul, and body, we cannot expect to live in peace and love unconditionally. Knowledge and understanding are the first steps toward the healing of damaged emotions.

A temporary treatment or a healing?

Techniques and therapies have their place in the healing process of the inner man, but if the emphasis is only on the treatments without the power of Christ Jesus to heal, transform, and set man free, it will be just that, a treatment that may or may not work.

Healing in the innermost of man is a miraculous process that only God, through His Holy Spirit, can manifest. Man can help a person normalize and suggest many things that are helpful and beneficial, but only God can heal. When God heals, man does not have to cope for the rest of his life but becomes a free person—free of the past, of guilt and condemnation, and free of his fears. The scars may remain, but God heals the wounds. And, like Jesus who carries His scars as a testimony of God's delivering power, we too all have scars that become our testimony of healing to help others in similar situations.

The transforming power of Christ is complete, setting a man free from emotional bondage, the past, abuse, offenses, and injustices. It focuses on the roots of the issues without digging into all the little details, without hypnosis and imaginary trips to *way down yonder*.

An encounter with the delivering power of Christ is powerful and spectacular, healing the soul of man, leaving behind a sweet aroma and going forward to a clean new start.

If you have a load of clothes to wash, you simply put them in the washer, add the detergent, set the dial, and let it wash till it's done. You don't spread the clothes out, investigate every little stitch, stain, and button, and then try to decide if they will shrink or fade out. No, you have an assurance that the washer will clean your clothes without tearing them apart or discoloring them.

We can trust God, who created us in His image, because He can set us free without tearing us apart or making us suffer the pain from the past all over again in order to help us recover. Once a person receives ministry and feels like a free person again, a desire awakens within to obey and serve God. He begins to experience a sense of well-being, more energy, and a better disposition. Fear is lifted from the person, and a desire to be positive takes its place. The things he couldn't and had no desire to do before, all of a sudden he is able to do effectively. A new level of understanding and desire for the Word of God begins to unfold as the person continues to walk in his freedom.

To really enjoy living in wholeness, free from an enslaving sin or a set negative and fearful pattern of thinking, we must have an understanding of the role our spirit, soul, and body play in the restoration and healing of our being. We must also understand that we have an enemy constantly looking to destroy our faith. If the enemy can steal your faith, he will also conquer your soul.

What Is the Role of Your Spirit?

The *spirit* is the life force of a person. It's the realm where his will, disposition, feelings, strength, enthusiasm, attitude, loyalty, influence, meaning, outlook in life, and moods are involved.

Our spirit is the area where perception, visions and dreams, and discovery of God's revelation and knowledge are attained. The spirit is the most profound part of our being. It is the area where we learn to discern God's truth and the lies of the devil.

The Holy Spirit of God in our spirit will teach us wisdom—good sense, wise decision making, and insight. He will teach us knowledge—specific information, facts, and data. He will also teach us understanding—interpretation, comprehension, and ability to understand.

The Bible mentions various different spirits, many of which are a hindrance to Christians battling with inner turmoil and brokenness. As you prayerfully read over this list, ask the Holy Spirit to reveal and help you understand if any of these spirits have become a stronghold, giving evil spirits demonic influence over some area in your life.

+ *Spirit of anguish* (tormented, suffering, painful, distressed, anxious, agonized)—Job 7:11
+ *Broken spirit* (inoperative, beaten, fragmented, shattered, no longer whole, weakened)—Job 17:1

+ *Compelling spirit* (convincing, persuasive, captivating, holding attention)—Job 32:18
+ *Spirit of deception* (misleading, lying, deceptive, dishonest, illusory, pretending, false)—1 Timothy 4:1
+ *Spirit of deep sleep* (slumber, inactive, postpone decisions, absorbed)—Isaiah 29:10
+ *Spirit of distress* (unsettled, worrying, stressful, painful, miserable)—1 Samuel 16:14–16
+ *Errant spirit* (wayward, sinful, delinquent, antisocial, offending, negligent)—Isaiah 29:24
+ *Spirit of error* (wrong belief, false assumption)—1 John 4:6
+ *Failing spirit* (deteriorated, weakened, dying, declining, inadequate)—Psalm 143:7
+ *Spirit of fear* (dread, terror, anxiety, worry, distress, panic attacks, apprehension)—2 Timothy 1:7
+ *Grieved spirit* (hurt, mourn, lament, saddened, distressed, intense sorrow)—Isaiah 65:14
+ *A hardened and obstinate spirit* (stubborn, refusing change, difficult to control, headstrong)—Deuteronomy 2:30
+ *Haughty spirit* (proud, arrogant, self-important, conceited)—Proverbs 16:18
+ *Spirit of heaviness* (needing strength, requiring concentration, lingering, oppressive)—Isaiah 61:3
+ *Human spirit* (our flesh)—Ezekiel 13:3
+ *Spirit of ill-will* (unkind, harmful, unfriendly, harsh, cruel)—Judges 9:23
+ *A spirit of jealousy* (envy, suspicion, distrust, possessiveness)—Numbers 5:14
+ *Overwhelmed spirit* (overcome emotionally, besieged, overpowered, devastated)—Psalm 142:3
+ *Perverse spirit* (obstinate, willful, stubborn, irrational, intentional, malicious)—Isaiah 19:14

- *Poisoned spirit* (disillusioned, polluted, infected, toxic, negative influence)—Job 6:4
- *Sorrowful spirit* (mournful, distressed, unhappy, sad, regretful, troubled)—1 Samuel 1:15
- *Sullen spirit* (hostile, dull, bad tempered, angry, gloomy, depressed)—1 Kings 21:5
- *Spirit turned against God* (contrary, opposed, conflict, in competition against)—Job 15:13
- *Unfaithful spirit* (disloyal, false, untrue, adulterous, faithless)—Psalm 78:8
- *Unruly spirit* (boisterous, disruptive, disorderly, disobedient, uncontrollable)—Proverbs 25:28
- *Unclean spirit* (impure, contaminated, unchaste, lustful, immoral, adulterated)—Matthew 10:1

Any one of these spirits can keep a person depressed, fearful, unstable, and unfruitful. It will be beneficial for you to do a study of the Scripture references of these spirits and seek the Holy Spirit to see if there are spirits working within you that may be the cause of hindrances and lack of peace and joy in your life.

The spirit of a person is susceptible and can be damaged. Trauma, abuse, neglect, uncertainty, and intense suffering can break the person's spirit and cause instability. Some of these adverse circumstances, through the course of a person's life, may cause the entrance of evil spirits, despondency, and uncontrollable desires.

Lack of self-control

The person who lacks control over her own spirit has trouble maintaining a normal and productive life and is easily tempted into immoral relationships and impulsiveness. Lack of self-control may also cause a person to become disorganized and scattered, quick-tempered, easily provoked, and unable to see or enjoy her God-given potential and abilities.

Results of brokenness to the human spirit

Suffering is a big issue today. Take a good look around you, and you will quickly notice anxiety, worry, panic attacks, depression, and all sorts of overwhelming situations affecting Christians and people who serve other gods.

Traumatic experiences, grieving, anguish, abandonment, and separation can adversely affect the human spirit. Only in the presence of God can we find healing and comfort. The Holy Spirit is ready and able to heal our brokenness. Nothing is too damaged or impossible for the blood of Jesus to heal. The price has already been paid at Calvary.

Trauma is defined as shock, upset, disturbance, ordeal, suffering, pain, distress, damage, and a lasting and strong negative impression. Its effect can be seen as flashbacks, bitterness, fearfulness, anxiety, a feeling of uselessness, and misery. The traumatized person is very needy, sincerely desiring healing and restoration, and sometimes may revert to his childhood. Only in the presence of God can a broken spirit be healed. It will be necessary for the person to get help from a mature prayer warrior who can pray a powerful prayer of healing and deliverance, setting the person free. The person must then follow in a guided prayer of release and cleansing, followed by teaching, accountability, and discipleship. Receiving freedom is a life-changing process— if done correctly and by knowledgeable servants of God, it will set the captives free.

A severely traumatized person should receive spiritual help from a trained counselor. I've prayed for many broken people and have seen the powerful results of deliverance and healing by the power of Almighty God in the name of Jesus. I do not recommend, nor have I ever practiced, trying to recover all the lost memories or digging into all the little details of the trauma or resurrecting the child within to produce evidence. You will find helpful and powerful model prayers and declarations at the end of each of the chapters of this book.

What Role Does the Soul Play
in a Person's Life?

The *soul* is the realm of the will, feelings, emotions, and spiritual perception. It's the area where the essence of heart issues surface and determine the actions of the person. It is from this realm the Bible says that the issues of life emerge and originate: "Keep your heart with all diligence, for out of it spring the issues of life" (Prov. 4:23).

The soul is like a warehouse of positive and negative emotions. The soul stores negative emotions—some provoked by wounds caused by our own decisions and mistakes, and some caused by other people we love. Many people may not be aware of the source of their torment.

Personal prisons

I consider a personal *spiritual prison* anything negative in the soul that hinders the person from enjoying salvation to the fullest. There are many reasons for negative emotions that may keep a person struggling for freedom:

+ Unfaithfulness by a marriage partner
+ Unfortunate circumstances or events such as death of a loved one, divorce, a great loss or disappointment, or a tragic event
+ Rejection from the womb provoked by a mother who was angry, not desiring to have a child at that time or attempting to unsuccessfully abort
+ Giving a child up for adoption, or a seed of rejection sown either from the womb or as a young child
+ Mental abuse in the form of personal rejection and ridicule
+ Sexual abuse, incest, and molestation caused by a loved one, a family member, or a stranger, which now has turned into a promiscuous habit or confusion of gender identity

- A deep hurt caused by words that were never pardoned
- A satanic ritual where a person or child is involved in a promise or sacrifice
- Curses passed down in the family by specific vows, oaths, and involvements in secret societies; curses passed down through involvement in séances, witchcraft, palm reading, psychic demonic involvement, sexual orgies, spoken by a parent or enemy; demonic board games
- Possession of amulets and trinkets, jewelry, signet rings, good luck charms, statues of other gods, books and artwork from foreign countries with demonic origin, religious souvenirs, beautiful secret society bibles and books passed down from one generation to the next

Evil spirit house intrusion

This reminds me of a small souvenir my husband brought home from his army tour in Vietnam. It was a one-inch-by-one-inch little wooden box, long forgotten and sitting in one of my husband's dresser drawers. A man of God visited our home, and as he prayed to bless our home, the Holy Spirit revealed to him that we had something in the home that invited evil spirits to come and go as they pleased. We looked at each other in amazement, unable to figure out what it could be. He prayed again and walked into our bedroom, opened the specific drawer, and took out the tiny wooden box. When he opened it, he exposed a meticulous tiny ivory carving of a Buddha god sitting in the center of half of a peach kernel giving the appearance of a throne. We were amazed that the Holy Spirit uncovered and paid such attention to such a small thing.

The real issue is not how big or how small or how forgotten the item may be. As the man of God explained, anything representing another deity or false god allowed in our home, our soul, and our space has the power to invade and disrupt our atmosphere, our thoughts, and, yes, even our feelings and emotions. Anything that is an idol or represents a demon, or is used to replace the true living God by acknowledgment or worship, is an abomination to God. The words out of his mouth as he looked at the tiny carving of the false god were, "His feet are on the ground and his head is in the clouds." In other words, this false god has lots of power to disrupt a person's life. It is an enemy and in opposition of the living God and an enemy of God's people.

A lot of Christians, including myself, can be ignorant of many things we bring into our homes and many things handed down by our ancestors. But another thought just pierced my mind...what are we allowing to invade our atmosphere and into our homes today? This is the modern high-tech global world where everything possible is accessible. We can order just about anything on eBay, Craigslist, or Amazon. Anything you want to know is obtainable at your fingertips with one stroke of a key. So, to the list above, I will have to add many things we Christians allow into our lives today that are unacceptable and abominable in God's sight. Perhaps you can think of some I may leave out.

Unclean things draw unclean spirits.

Unclean movies, permissive reality shows, videos, and games portraying violence, porn, foul language, infidelity, desperate people, lust, unclean romance novels, child abuse, bisexuality, and so forth—*ouuuch!* "But...everybody does it!" These issues alone, without getting into all the other stuff Christians dabble with, are one of the answers or reasons why we have such a high percentage of rebellious children and teens, rampant infidelity, divorce, and emotionally strung-out and depressed people. It would take me an entire book just to deal with this taboo, out-of-bounds, and socially acceptable and tolerant subject.

I really want to admonish God's people, as a spiritual mother, that the time of accountability is coming when God is separating the sheep from the goats (Matt. 25:31–33). God is bound by His Word, and He cannot bless ungodliness. The time is now here when with our own eyes we will see God's hand of mercy extended to everyone who dares to forsake iniquity and love God and others with a pure unadulterated heart. The believers who know the truth and turn their backs by fulfilling the desires of their flesh are already witnessing a dwindling down of their effectiveness and their substance.

Unclean and lingering spirits from any of the above issues can hold a person prisoner and unstable until the person recognizes where the attacks and irrational emotions are stemming from. As soon as the person takes action to clean house and oust and bring captive all demonic strongholds in the name of Jesus, all hindering, unclean, and lingering spirits *must* leave the believer. A recognizable peace takes over. A desire to stay clean and make changes becomes a priority. The need to keep the mind occupied with God's Word and pure thoughts is key and imperative to obtain complete healing.

Your personal *prison* may be one of those mentioned above or something else still entrenched in the core of your being. Your *prison* may be that you've been deprived of your children, your respect and honor, your place in your home, or your value. Perhaps you may be angry all the time, cussing and swearing and damning everything you feel obligated to do. I consider a spiritual prison anything that a person has experienced or is experiencing that is still a source of preoccupation and distress, and, many times, torment.

> Bring my soul out of prison,
> That I may praise Your name;
> The righteous shall surround me,
> For You shall deal bountifully with me.
>
> —PSALM 142:7

Perhaps you find yourself imprisoned between the *sword and the wall*—a miserable, hard place of constant harassment. Your life is not what you desired and imagined. Your dreams of a wonderful marriage and good kids are now a collage of uncertainty and devastation. You haven't left because you have nowhere to go and no money to make it on your own, or perhaps your strong deep-rooted religious convictions have you in a place of no return. Perhaps you have everything you need: a wonderful house, car, clothes, lots of things, but no freedom to enjoy it. Your spouse is jealous and suspicious all the time. You have no life of your own, and you're not content. I sincerely pray that you will experience healing and wholeness as you apply the principles and prayers in this book.

Spirits of anger, hate, resentment, condemnation

King David said, "A happy heart is good medicine and a cheerful mind works healing, but a broken spirit dries up the bones" (Prov. 17:22, AMP).

Your mind and intellect can have an intense and profound influence on your spirit and physical body. Your mind (thoughts and memories) will also affect your spiritual knowledge and general quality of life. The mind, body, and spirit are all uniquely interconnected. When one is affected, all are affected. We may be able to live a healthy lifestyle and perform our spiritual duties, but if the mind is not functioning well, eventually the person may suffer a breakdown.

I remember when I was in my own prison of hate and unforgiveness. I hated my father so much I wished him dead every day. For many years after the child abuse I experienced, I imagined him dead in a car accident. To forgive him was totally out of the question. A few years after I was married, I received valuable teaching about soul healing and transformation. I learned that hate is a stronghold that would keep me in prison as long as I allowed it. I also learned that if I allowed God to heal my heart, I would have the capacity to forgive my father. I realized I was a prisoner, and I desired to really be free. When I finally surrendered my life and my burdens to God, and I said a prayer asking God to forgive my father and forgive me for hating him, I experienced a deep release and a sense of well-being. I came out of prison! From then on I was different. The change and transformation healed my emotions and opened the doors of blessing, not only for me but for my household as well.

Thoughts and words are powerful. When they leave your mouth, they have action in them—for good or for evil. When my father cursed my mom and threatened to murder her and the children, he sent out powerful evil words into the atmosphere. Satan heard them, and God heard them. Mom had power with God. She's a prayer warrior, a woman of God. That same day a car struck my father as he crossed the street. He remained a quadriplegic for fourteen years before he died. Dad had every opportunity to surrender his life to God and receive healing of his soul and spirit, but he refused the healing. An unsurrendered soul is exposed to every form of evil spirits.

Quick action is necessary to receive restoration and cleansing from the foul spirits of anger, hate, resentment, and condemnation, otherwise they will make abode in the soul and cause destructive emotions to hinder your walk with God. Freedom from these spirits will cause physical and mental healing to begin its work of restoration. If left untended, these spirits are the roots of many behavioral, emotional, and physical disorders such as depression, stress, frustration, anxiety, panic attacks, phobias, nervous breakdowns, and sickness.

Many other emotional disorders—such as addictions to gambling, codependency, compulsive obsession, unhappiness, abandonment, eating disorders, compulsive shopping, and addiction to sex and pornography—can be instigated by evil spirits that keep the person fixated. There is much research out there verifying that emotional stress, once unbridled, can cause illness, including cancer and immune system diseases.

Coming out of a spiritual prison

Many people walk through life wearing a mask, giving the impression of success, when in reality the walls of the human spirit are broken down. Some may have already tried many things to get well, and like the woman in the Bible with the issue of blood, they are still suffering. The only way to receive lasting healing is in God's presence. The blood of Jesus has already purchased our salvation and our healing. Read the scriptures and pray the prayers at the end of this chapter. *Healing of your soul is something God wants to do right now!*

Once a person knows in his heart that he's been restored and renewed and a weight has lifted, he has come out of a spiritual prison. At this point, depending on the depth of turmoil and suffering experienced by the person receiving the healing, the process of sanctification must begin together with biblical training for transformation of character. If necessary, seek help from a knowledgeable and anointed minister or Christian counselor with experience in the area of deliverance from evil spirits.

If professional counseling is necessary, the person should never feel controlled or intimidated by his counselor. I've seen several cases where the person experienced dread and panic attacks when the counselor had to go on a trip or a vacation. The thought of separation from the counselor caused fear and desperation to build up in the counselee. This is definitely not the way the Holy Spirit heals a person. The miracle in all this is that the presence of God is the invisible agent that pours out the healing into the broken soul. God's living water begins cleansing immediately.

What Role Does the Body Perform in the Spiritual Realm?

The body is the physical form of a human. It is the container where the spirit and soul reside. If the body is always tired, sick, overextended, sluggish, and malnourished, it is very difficult for the spirit (the realm of your will and your soul and the area of your feelings and heart issues) to pay attention or desire serving a God you cannot see, much less desire to do what is right.

We must take care of our body, or it will slow us down and take the joy out of living.

Not only will a sluggish and malnourished body find it difficult to enjoy and pay attention to the things of the Spirit of God, but it will also find it difficult or impossible to ward off the attacks of the enemy.

Radical healing and change can only be accomplished through the saving grace of Jesus. We can reach out to help people by encouraging them to repent and confess their sins. We can teach them forgiveness and the freedom of living a guilt- and shame-free life. We can help them through counseling and different kinds of psychiatric therapies, but unless supernatural divine intervention takes place, it will be only a temporary fix.

Once a person accepts the new birth in Christ Jesus and receives discipleship and an understanding of Romans chapter 6, the Holy Spirit will do the work of restoration in the person. The more understanding and practice a person receives about the process of cleansing and forsaking of the old personality and nature, the stronger, healthier, and more content the person will become.

Jesus came to restore men and women created in His image from sin, sickness, and broken hearts. Unspoken and unconfessed sin will always keep the person under an immense burden of emotional grief. Too many broken people are so focused on themselves that they are unable to see Father God waiting to miraculously heal them.

THE GIFT OF REPENTANCE AND FORGIVENESS

Repentance and forgiveness are two special gifts God has made available to break the power of Satan over us. Sin is a deadly trap that enslaves and chokes the life out of its victim. It is a slow death. When I repent of all the things I consciously know do not please God, and I forgive and receive forgiveness, I must believe deep down in my heart that God accepts me as His daughter and that I instantly become clean and accepted by the Father as His own. I must determine to thrive and go forward with my life.

Inner transformation of the soul is a step-by-step process. The person doesn't have to bring to memory every minute detail of his past and all the bad things that transpired. God established repentance and forgiveness as the necessary process for healing of the spirit, soul, and body. God knew that without establishing these two priorities, a person would forever be spiritually handicapped.

Discipleship and recovery

It is interesting to me that a lot of Christians readily learn from bold men and women of God how to make positive declarations, decree abundance and prosperity, and sacrificially make vows and promises to seal their confessions and prophetic words, but they neglect to seek out help for the healing of their emotional and spiritual disorders. This too, I believe, is not as much their fault as it is the lack of discipleship and understanding in this area.

My church, Calvary Church in Irving, Texas, has a wonderful Celebrate Recovery program. I believe every church needs to offer classes for the restoration of the soul. Too many people are coming in to Christianity seeking salvation and help from a life of abuse and crisis, and they are not receiving enough teaching and guidance to restore what the enemy, ignorance, and curses have stolen from them.

A visit to church on Sundays, an occasional inspirational concert, or listening to a special motivational speaker will not do the work of the Holy Spirit in the heart of someone who really needs help to heal from the emotional trauma so many people drag around all the time.

To receive healing, a person must believe in his heart that God truly loves him. God's love is healing. Satan gains power over an unprotected heart by influencing the mind of his followers. God's unconditional love is able and willing to restore all that Satan has perverted. Christ Jesus paid the price to redeem us from the curse of spiritual death and to exchange a broken heart with a new heart. (See Ezekiel 11:19; 18:31; 36:26; 2 Corinthians 3:3.)

CLOSE THE DOOR!

The Word of God reveals the truth. Healing of our bodies is dependent on the healing of our souls. Studies done by health professionals conclude that unforgiveness, resentment, hatred, and bitterness can cause many diseases. Negative attitudes, whether in the mind or emotions, can give an open door and a right for the devil to attack our physical bodies (Eph. 4:26–27). Once a person obeys God and forgives those who have hurt him, he finds it easier to receive and maintain healing—it all begins in the soul. The apostle John wrote: "Beloved, I pray that you may prosper in all things and be in health, just as your soul prospers" (3 John 2).

INSTRUCTIONS AND PRAYERS TO RECEIVE SOUL HEALING AND TRANSFORMATION

When truth penetrates our thoughts, faith leaps into our spirits. Faith releases the power of God to heal and restore our souls.

Go to a secret place. Get ready to bare your heart and surrender yourself to God. Be transparent. Don't be afraid. Say: "In the name of Jesus, I cast fear out of my heart!"

Now say this prayer:

> *Heavenly Father, I surrender myself to You right now. I admit that I need Your help. I've messed up in many ways, and I repent of all disobedience and acts of my will that have taken me out of Your protection and blessings. I humbly ask for Your forgiveness. Cleanse me now, and renew a right spirit within me. Thank You, Father God, for transforming my soul and having mercy on me.*

> But if we walk in the light as He is in the light, we have fellowship with one another, and the blood of Jesus Christ His Son cleanses us from all sin. If we say that we have no sin, we deceive ourselves, and the truth is not in us. If we confess our sins, He is faithful and just to forgive us our sins and to cleanse us from all unrighteousness.
>
> —1 JOHN 1:7–9

Prayer

Dear Lord Jesus, I desire to really know You and the depth of Your love for me. Today I open my heart and welcome You completely into my life, asking You to heal all my painful situations and memories, as well as all the brokenness and traumatic experiences of my past. You alone are the light of the world, my Savior and Lord. Have mercy on me. I surrender my life and my will to You. Please cleanse and forgive me of all sins and iniquities. Heal and sanctify every area of my spirit, soul, and body that has been controlled and tormented by evil spirits. I declare that Jesus is my Lord and my Healer. I plead the blood of Jesus over my spirit, soul, and body.

I now renounce the power of Satan over my life and my destiny. I declare that Jesus Christ is my Lord! Today I declare that I am FREE! No weapon formed against me shall prosper [Isa. 54:17]. Fear no longer has any place in me. I cast fear out of my heart! The love of God now rules my heart. I will submit myself to God. I will resist the devil, and he must flee from me. I release all guilt and condemnation accusing me. Thank You, my Lord, because I am in Christ, and I will walk according to the Spirit of the Lord. In the name of Jesus Christ, amen!

PRAYERS AND SCRIPTURES TO COME OUT OF SPIRITUAL PRISONS

Bring my soul out of prison,
That I may praise Your name;
The righteous shall surround me,
For You shall deal bountifully with me.

—PSALM 142:7

Father, thank You for bringing my soul out of prison. Thank You for setting me free from the poison of bitterness and iniquity [Acts 8:23]. Father, I know You dearly love me, and You desire to see me whole. You have given us the gift of Jesus Christ as a covenant to open our spiritual eyes and bring prisoners out of torment and darkness. Thank You, my Lord, for giving me understanding and delivering me out of the personal prisons that have kept me from enjoying my salvation [Isa. 42:6–7]. *Father God, thank You for healing me and restoring everything that I have been unable to enjoy. Thank You for bringing me out of the wilderness and blessing my life with Your love* [Isa. 43:18–19].

For God has not given us a spirit of fear, but of power and of love and of a sound mind.

—2 TIMOTHY 1:7

Father, I will submit to God. I will resist the devil, and he must flee from me. Thank You for this promise [James 4:7]. *I thank You, Father, because I'm no longer under guilt and condemnation. Through Jesus I have the righteousness of God in me! I'm not hoping to be healed sometime in the future, but I believe the Word of God that by His stripes I have already been healed* [Isa. 53:5]. *Body and soul, get in line with God's Word! It is God's will that I prosper in all things and be in good health, just as my soul prospers.*

If you're in need of salvation, please go to the last chapter of this book and confess the salvation prayer.

CHAPTER TWO

THE MIRACLE OF DELIVERANCE FROM EVIL

Don't you realize that you become the slave of whatever you choose to obey? You can be a slave to sin, which leads to death, or you can choose to obey God, which leads to righteous living.

—ROMANS 6:16, NLT

I BELIEVE THAT A person unknowingly can yield an area of her life to a demonic stronghold, for instance, victims of sexual abuse. Others, through repetition, willingly yield to temptation. When a person repeatedly yields her body to sin and iniquity, that person becomes a slave to sin, which leads to spiritual death. There are many temptations and sins that beset Christians. People in this condition wonder why God doesn't answer their prayers and why they continue struggling with the same sins. It doesn't mean they are demon possessed, but I believe that a demonic influence is at work. The person may love and serve God with all her heart but still struggle with something she despises and knows doesn't please God. Others have totally forsaken their past, but they still find themselves struggling with invisible forces.

Major areas of demonic involvement include the following sins:

- *Sexual sins*—such as adultery, fornication, prostitution, sexual lust, incest, rape, spousal abuse and perversion, and others
- *Sins of the soul*—such as unforgiveness, jealousy, rage, anger, hate, and lying

+ *Sins of tolerance*—such as drug and alcohol addiction, glut-
    tony, and insatiable desires

Some of the real-life examples of demonic involvement that I am
highlighting here are intended to get my point across with clarity
about this subject. It is important for Christians to understand how
easy and subtle it is to become entangled by the enemy. I also want
to expose some of the areas that may be hindering some people from
receiving their healing and living a victorious life no matter how hard
they try. At the end of this chapter you will find prayers, scriptures,
and declarations that will help you walk in freedom if you sincerely
want help. Hebrews 4:12 declares that, "The Word that God speaks
is alive and full of power [making it active, operative, energizing, and
effective]" (AMP).

DELIVERANCE FROM WITCHCRAFT
AND WORSHIP TO OTHER GODS

It is no secret that Mexico has been embattled in a deathly war of wide-
spread homicides, drugs, kidnappings, mass murders, and horrendous
gang wars for many years. There are many reasons Satan has gained
a foothold in this country and in many other countries that are going
through turbulence. One of them is the worship of other gods and the
practice of witchcraft. I happen to love the Mexican people. My husband and I have many Christian ministers and friends living there, and
we minister in different places at least twice a year. It is amazing to
see how well the rapidly growing body of Christians flourish and keep
their sanity in the midst of so much chaos and vandalism. You may
live in a hellhole, but God's love and His favor will sustain you. I am a
living testimony of His amazing love.

A few months ago my husband was ministering in the ravished
city of Juarez, Mexico, and our host pastor related the story of how in
2006 a celebration took place where many of the lower classes openly
paraded a demon named *Santa Muerte* (saint of holy death), which

many of these people embrace as their patron saint. Soon afterward an alarming increase in homicides began to take place. Gang leaders started inciting demonic warfare among one another, taking over neighborhoods, holding up business owners, and murdering whoever got in their way. The result to date has been extreme devastation, mass murders, and dreadful fear. A large number of business owners have opted to leave the city and abandon their businesses, many totally devastated and stripped of all their substance and livelihood. Poverty, sickness, disease, and incredible fear have replaced the once thriving city.

It is a known fact that this demonic entity is a stronghold in many cities of Mexico and other parts of the world, especially among the poor. Their belief is that this death saint is very powerful and able to protect them from all evil, grant their wishes, and even ward off the attacks of Satan. Followers are also persuaded into believing that if they break allegiance or try to defect, they can face death, ill favor, accidents, barrenness, and bad luck, not only to them but to their family members as well. Most people under this curse and stronghold are very fearful and continue serving this demonic stronghold because they fear death and retaliation.

The cult is condemned by the Catholic Church in Mexico, but it is firmly entrenched among Mexico's lower classes and criminal worlds. The number of believers in *Santa Muerte* has grown over the past ten to twenty years, to approximately two million followers, and has crossed the border into Mexican American communities in the United States.[1]

Divine intervention will be necessary to unseat and dethrone demonic strongholds at work not only in Mexico but also in so many other cities and countries of the world.

Defeating a demonic stronghold begins with knowledge.

Defeating this or any other kind of demonic stronghold has to begin by applying wisdom, knowledge, and understanding. People have to be trained and disciplined about the true living God, the kingdom of heaven, and the sacrifice Jesus paid on the cross of Calvary to redeem mankind and defeat Satan. The lie has to be supplanted by truth. *Ignorance and fear activates the influence of the demonic.*

A bold determination and spiritual warfare have to be kindled in the hearts of all believers, for there are many cowering in fear. Prayer has to be specific, targeted, and consistent. Everything representing other gods and secret practices with the dark world should be burned and renounced. Coming out of demonic bondage is a miraculous event. Only God Almighty can deliver and set a captive free.

Once a demonic principality becomes enthroned as a fortress in the life of a person, family, or group of people, destruction and pestilence quickly follow. I believe this is one of the reasons why there is so much poverty and famine in so many parts of the world today. Worship to other gods and the practice of witchcraft, sorcery, and everything that is an abomination to God will always keep people, families, neighborhoods, cities, and nations who practice it under a heavy burden of slavery, famine, and fear. (See Exodus 20:3-5.)

Is witchcraft and demonism openly propagated in the Western world and other progressive countries, or is this practice only common in developing nations? The answer is absolutely yes! In fact, it's becoming an accepted trend to dabble in witchcraft, go to palm readers, read occult-related material, and watch the latest gory and demonic thrillers. Even the recent cheap thrillers are reaping the highest attendance, surpassing very expensive and professional motion pictures.

What causes this hunger for the occult and supernatural?

Something occult is secret, hidden, difficult to see, and magical. The supernatural is something related to deity—not of the natural world, but mystic, ghostly, paranormal, weird, uncanny, and bizarre. It awakens the curiosity of the person. It causes the heart to race and the adrenaline to run wild. Many watch and participate in fear and ignorance, but they keep getting drawn into the unknown until Satan has a solid grip and uses them at his will.

The fact is that we are spiritual beings. When we look at each other, we see the physical dressing, but we can't see the spirit or discern what's in the heart. Demons or spirits are evil spirit beings that have no body. One of their goals is to have a human host to express their will and personality in the natural world and to use the person to lead other people into demonic slavery. If they can't find a living host, they can attach themselves to objects especially dedicated to that purpose, such as idols, amulets, charms, fetishes, or instruments of ritualistic worship. They can also inhabit physical locations such as a building, house, or an area within a house. Satan has an organized kingdom, just as God has the kingdom of heaven.

Why am I including this subject of deliverance from evil in this book about the miraculous power of God? Because Satan also works miracles to keep enslaving people into his kingdom. And because many Christians are still suffering attacks from the enemy, and they have no idea how to set themselves free. Our Western theology makes little room for the study of deliverance from evil. Many people don't want to mess with anything that has to do with demonism. Ignorance keeps people suffering. To become free, action, knowledge, and faith are necessary.

God instructed His people to keep His Words (teachings, principles, guidelines, instructions, laws, and decrees) and to study, read, and apply them until they penetrate deep into their heart and soul. We must enthrone God in our hearts and homes. We must learn all about the kingdom of heaven and teach these principles to our children. If we don't, they will grow up and become attracted to the kingdom of Satan with all its mysterious trappings and demonic allurements.

> Therefore you shall lay up these words of mine in your heart and in your soul, and bind them as a sign on your hand, and they shall be as frontlets between your eyes. You shall teach them to your children, speaking of them when you sit in your house, when you walk by the way, when you lie down, and when you rise up. And you shall write them on the doorposts of your house and on your gates, that

your days and the days of your children may be multiplied
in the land of which the Lord swore to your fathers to give
them, like the days of the heavens above the earth.
—DEUTERONOMY 11:18–21

The devil takes hold of a legal spiritual principle and converts and
usurps it to deceive and enslave people. The devil uses deception in
everything he does. People are deceived because they have no knowledge or understanding of God's principles.

HEALING FROM BARRENNESS

About three years ago we ministered in a Spirit-filled Hispanic church
in Texas. The pastor is one of our spiritual sons. During the altar ministry many people came for prayer. Before my husband prayed for the
people, he led them in a prayer of commitment to God and renunciation to all demonic power inherited or from anything in their past.
Two women came up asking for prayer to be able to conceive. They had
been barren for many years, and doctors could not explain why they
were unable to have children. One of them had three consecutive mis-
carriages. She even consulted with a witch doctor and fortune-teller,
but they told her the spirit of death was over her and they couldn't
help her. My husband prayed a powerful prayer with authority, commanding all demonic strongholds and curses to release the two women,
pleading the blood of Jesus over them and asking God to bless them
with children. A few months later their pastor called to happily inform
us that both women had become pregnant. We had great faith that
God would answer our prayers as He has done so many times.

About three months ago we were invited to minister in the same
church. The pastor wanted us to meet the two women and their young
children. They were elated and thankful that God had intervened in
their situation. But this is what I really want to impress upon you.
The woman with the spirit of death over her testified that many years
ago she had been influenced by the demon spirit of *Santa Muerte*. She

remembers that when she was a child, her mother placed a small altar of this demon in her room for protection. Constant fear was her companion until the day she accepted Jesus Christ as her Savior. As the years went by, she realized she was unable to conceive even though she was growing in her walk with God. These women had been receiving Bible teaching from their pastor and were now ready to receive deliverance. A powerful prayer of deliverance, commanding the evil spirits to release them from barrenness was made, and shortly afterward they were able to conceive.

That evening we heard of many other testimonies of deliverance from the curse of this demonic stronghold and from other forms of witchcraft. One man testified that he was suffering from a piercing pain in his side that attacked him at night for several years, and when his pastor led him in a prayer of renunciation and deliverance, the pain totally disappeared.

Demons seek to enslave people, just as they themselves are also bond slaves to Satan. They enslave a person to destructive emotions such as fear, rage, anger, and hatred. Many people under demonic influence have destructive habits such as drug abuse, alcohol addiction, and sexual sins. Demons incite thoughts of greed, envy, perversion, lust, and many others. *Believers have to pay attention to some of these emotions encouraged by the flesh as well, and which can also open the door to demonic enslavement.*

> Let's not kid ourselves. Whitney Houston was not the only person who talked about Jesus yet struggled privately with illegal drugs. I frequently meet men and women at church altars who have never found the strength to kick their habit. I even know of pastors, youth leaders, and worship leaders who live double lives—hiding their addiction under the cloak of Sunday morning religion. They hide because they're afraid they'll be shunned or shamed if they ever admit their problem to anybody.
>
> What we need is less judgment and more transparency

about this problem. Drugs, including alcohol, are harsh taskmasters. Crack and crystal meth are impossible to overcome apart from serious intervention. Once a person's brain is altered by these substances, he or she needs a miracle. Telling them to "Just say no" is not going to cut it....If you are addicted, please be willing to seek help by admitting your problem to your pastor or a trusted Christian friend. If you have someone in your family who is addicted, don't wait until it's too late to intervene. Barge into their lives if necessary to show tough love....Remember: Jesus has a message for anyone struggling with drugs: "Come to me, all who are weary and heavy-laden, and I will give you rest" (Matt. 11:28, NAS). Whitney Houston's death was tragic, but perhaps the warning that emerges from her story will end up saving lives.[2]

THINGS THAT INVITE DEMONIC SPIRITS

Is there something in your life and home inviting demonic spirits? Today we allow so many ungodly things to enter our homes. Our lives are being affected by everything that is unholy, opening doors to rebellion, disobedience, promiscuity, and the realm of defiant evil spirits. Unfortunately it's not only what we allow into our homes, but it's also what adults are modeling in today's Christian home. Many allow violent movies and indecent entertainment, telling small children to *cover their eyes* until the violent or indecent episode is over. I know couples who constantly fight over this issue. The husband wants to see the violent and explicit videos, and the wife wants no part of it.

The effects of tolerating and inviting ungodly stuff into your home may at first seem subtle, as both adults and children start demonstrating a little anger, a little pouting, a little nagging, a little impatience and annoyance, a little rebellion, a little disrespect, and a little lying and testing of the boundaries. But as time goes by, it goes from a little to a lot of episodes of self-will and emotional displays. Where children are involved, many of today's parents are too busy and harried to deal with the attention and accountability necessary to enforce rules or keep a hand on the wheel. Tough love seems to be a thing of the past in many families of this generation.

One of the greatest outcomes of all this permissiveness is the disintegration of the Christian home. Every day I receive e-mails from spouses who read my books *Satan, You Can't Have My Marriage* and *Satan, You Can't Have My Children,* and the number one complaint from wives is that their husbands are having affairs or messing with pornography. The main complaint from men is that their wives are controlling and manipulative and won't submit to even the most basic areas of respect and honor to which the Word of God so wisely instructs a wife to adhere.

Both of these areas, *pornography* and *manipulation,* are controlled by evil spirits. Spiritual cleansing and deliverance are absolutely necessary to become free from these demonic spirits that break up homes and churches. Believe it or not, too many Christians are involved in pornography, and many couples manipulate each other unaware of the lurking evil spirits behind their actions. Too many religious women refuse to submit to their husbands, bossing them around and correcting everything they do and say. This too is a root of manipulation and control.

God wants to heal His people so they can live in victory.

The Bible says that we have been given "authority...over all the power of the enemy, and nothing shall by any means hurt you" (Luke 10:19). Ignorance about this teaching will keep a Christian oblivious of Satan's devices. As we use our authority over the enemy and believe the Word of God in obedience, the power of the Holy Spirit takes care of the cleanup job. *It's not by might nor by power, but by the Spirit of the Lord* that demons have to obey the command of a believer (Zech. 4:6).

I like the way Pastor Bill Johnson describes the words *power* and *authority.*

Authority is quite different from power. Power is explosive and environmental in the sense it is the actual atmosphere of heaven that changes the atmosphere of earth. Authority is a position given by Jesus Himself. A policeman carries a gun (power), but he also carries a badge (authority). The badge does much more than the gun. Power is the atmosphere of heaven. Ministering in power is like catching a wave. Authority is like starting a wave. Things start happening because of who God says we are and what our responsibilities are. Faith is what connects us to this realm of authority—we have to believe what He says about us and what He has commissioned us to do.[3]

Satan has devised his own specific campaign strategies for blinding our young adults to become fascinated by the aura and magic of the dark and occult spirit world, as he draws troves of our young people into spiritual death and uncertainty. He is also blinding married couples into believing that if things get messy and love is blurry, they can easily divorce and go on with someone else. Lust is consuming people in all echelons of life, whether married, single, or divorced. Today's blended family is struggling with multiple volatile problems. How can a Christian live in victory and under God's blessing when so many unresolved soul issues are still waiting to be healed?

Evidence of demonic involvement

I personally know a young Christian woman—not just any girl, but one reared in a good Christian home and who attained excellent grades and was actively involved in her college education—charged with premeditated murder and serving a life sentence after killing a young college classmate because of jealousy. Jealousy (envy, suspicion, protectiveness, mistrust, possessiveness) is a tormenting spirit armed with destruction. Once evil spirits are allowed to develop roots in the heart, the oppressed person needs a miracle of divine intervention to expel them. The mind of the troubled person must be renewed by filling it with the Word of God and bringing down strongholds to the obedience of God.

When lots of impure and negative thinking and imaginations are allowed into the mind and heart of a person, the Spirit of God is pushed out, and the person acts independently of the leading and protection of the Holy Spirit. I hope I am getting this important point across clearly. Believers who are desperately struggling to maintain a relationship with God while at the same time battling with disturbing habits they know are wrong, but they feel helpless to overcome, must learn how to cooperate with God. Otherwise their Christianity will always feel like a constant desperate battle.

It is astonishing that as I write, I took a break to see the news and was faced with more alarming headlines of men and children committing horrendous acts of murder.

> A central Missouri teenager who confessed to strangling, cutting and stabbing a 9-year-old girl because she wanted to know how it felt to kill someone was sentenced Wednesday to life in prison with the possibility of parole....
>
> "I know words," she said, pausing to take a deep breath and struggling to compose herself, "can never be enough and they can never adequately describe how horribly I feel for all of this."
>
> She added: "If I could give my life to get her back I would. I'm sorry."...
>
> The teenager's defense attorneys had argued for a sentence less than life in prison, saying Bustamante's use of the antidepressant Prozac had made her more prone to violence. They said she had suffered from depression for years and once attempted suicide by overdosing on painkillers....
>
> Missouri State Highway Patrol Sgt. David Rice testified that the teenager told him "she wanted to know what it felt like" to kill someone. Prosecutors also cited journal

entries in which Bustamante described the exhilaration of killing Elizabeth...

"It was ahmazing. As soon as you get over the 'ohmygawd I can't do this' feeling, it's pretty enjoyable. I'm kinda nervous and shaky though right now. Kay, I gotta go to church now...lol."

Bustamante then headed off to a youth dance at her church while a massive search began for the missing girl.[4]

What really disturbs me is that both of these young women were connected to a church and had the opportunity to receive help if they had asked for help or if someone had noticed. A person oppressed by an evil spirit does irrational things when strongholds of unmet needs and unresolved hurts are triggered by an emotional event. These young ladies needed counsel, training, and discipleship. They also needed someone mature and fearless in prayer to address the strongholds and speak life and healing into their lives.

Deliverance means to release, free, and rescue. When a person accepts Jesus Christ as Lord and Savior and truly believes she has been transferred from the kingdom of darkness into the kingdom of light, she can't stop there. Now begins the process of transformation and cleansing from all evil, the past, inherited curses and strongholds, and the renewing of the mind. *This is a miraculous process, for only the Spirit of God can indwell a man or woman and cause this great transformation.* Evil spirits who once occupied the person before salvation will try to come back to see if the person's soul is still empty, or if faith and the Word of God are occupying the person (Matt. 12:43–45). The scriptures and declarations at the end of this chapter will greatly help people build up their spiritual defenses and fill their spiritual house.

THE MIRACLE OF DELIVERANCE FROM CURSES

> No man can enter into a strong man's house, and spoil his
> goods, except he will first bind the strong man; and then he
> will spoil his house.
>
> —MARK 3:27, KJV

The Greek word for *spoil* in this scripture is *diarpazō*, which means "to plunder, seize, or snatch away." The Greek word for "house" is *oikos*, meaning "dwelling place." To reverse the curse, you must learn how to spoil the house of the demon(s) involved in the curse. Satan may think that your house, your mate, your children, and your substance belong to him, and he may threaten to steal, kill, and destroy what is legally yours, but God has made provision for your deliverance from the destruction of the enemy.

After many years of practicing spiritual warfare, I know that I cannot simply *bind* the work of the enemy and guarantee total victory. You must totally "spoil" his house, for he's always looking for a way back in, especially when a person lets his or her guard down in an area of weakness.

God said to the prophet Jeremiah: "See, I have this day set you over the nations and over the kingdoms, to root out and to pull down, to destroy and to throw down, to build and to plant" (Jer. 1:10). Jeremiah was instructed to destroy and eradicate all roots of evil strongholds and idol worship by severing and destroying its growth and proliferation. A stronghold is any area controlled by evil spirits such as addictions, damaging habits, and out-of-control emotions. It may be tendencies toward violent or criminal behavior known to be a generational stronghold in the family. Satan gains control in families through sin, iniquity, and generational curses. It is only when a born-again believer spoils the strongholds and roots out and destroys every area of demonic influence that Satan must release his control. *Immediately* the soul must be renewed by building a new spiritual foundation and planting the Word of God in the heart.

Don't take this subject lightly. Curses are real and emotionally damage a lot of people and families. They are not only emotional outbursts, but also defiant and powerful acts that affect every fiber of the person. More and more people in our culture are involved in occult practices where they invoke curses and take secret oaths that may produce sickness, despair, barrenness, failure, loss, divorce, and accidents. When many of these people receive salvation, they continue experiencing the effects of their past involvements.

HOW TO DESTROY STRONGHOLDS AND CURSES

How do we destroy, spoil, and sever the roots of demonic strongholds and curses? Our heavenly Father made provision for all those who accept and believe in the Lord Jesus Christ and who dwell under the protection of the blood of Jesus to break themselves and others free from the yoke of self-imposed and generational curses. To be set free, the following steps are important:

- *Take heed* (pay attention to advice, be mindful, observe) to do according to God's Word. Live a morally clean life. Remain steadfast, obeying God's Word so that Satan is unable to cross the line (Ps. 119:9; Prov. 26:2; Mal. 4:6).
- *Dress yourself every day with the full armor of God.* Keep your mind focused on God's Word. Speak, pray, meditate, and confess the Word. Stay out of the places that bring temptation and confusion and wrong relationships. Protect your feet. Protect your mouth. Protect your heart. The Word of God is a flaming sword to combat the enemy (Eph. 6:10–20).
- *Plead the blood of Jesus.* We conquer by the blood of Jesus and the word of our testimony. When Jesus died on the cross of Calvary, He set us free from the dominion of sin and the power of the enemy. His blood guarantees our access to God and releases us from the bondage of Satan.

Christ became a curse for us so that we could be free from all curses (Rev. 12:11; Gal. 3:10–14).

+ *Do not participate in any sins involving occult practices,* idol worship, ceremonies, or family traditions that involve any kind of satanic worship. Cleanse your heart by praying yourself clean with the Word of God.

+ *Destroy and get rid of all evil objects,* amulets, trinkets, jewelry, keepsakes, and artwork associated with pagan worship and the occult.

+ *Join a prayer and discipleship group* in a Bible-based and Spirit-filled church. Feed your mind on the Word of God.

Putting the information together for this chapter was accomplished by divine intervention. It has not been easy. Satan does not want this information to get out. Much prayer and vigilance has covered every word in this manuscript. If you need help and healing, or if someone you know needs healing, please follow the instructions and counsel carefully and determine in your heart to allow the Holy Spirit to set you free. As I completed this section, a computer bug blanked out my document, and I lost valuable time and much editing. But praise God, the bulk of it was sitting in my drop box. Everything good will cost you something. Determine in your heart to serve your Creator with all your heart. God Almighty is the true living God, and He won't tolerate any other gods before Him. His blessings and treasures are for His children who obey Him.

PRAYERS, SCRIPTURES, AND DECLARATIONS TO SET YOU FREE FROM CURSES, DEMONIC STRONGHOLDS, AND ATTACKS OF THE ENEMY

Father, Your Word declares that Jesus disarmed all principalities and powers of Satan when He willingly died on the cross to redeem us, and because He triumphed over them, I am no longer a slave to the devil's devices [Col. 2:14–15].

Father, thank You for the authority and promise You have given us to trample and defeat evil spirits, and over all the power of the enemy. Nothing shall by any means hurt us [Luke 10:19].

Father, thank You because in Christ we have redemption through His blood, and the forgiveness of sins, according to the riches of His grace [Eph. 1:7].

Father, thank You for this great promise that Christ has redeemed us from the curse of the law, having become a curse for us, that we might receive the promise of the Spirit through faith [Gal. 3:13–14].

Dissolve agreements and curses by confessing the following prayers

These are simple, breakthrough prayers and to the point. Don't underestimate the tremendous power to be set free when you make these declarations. If you're not married, say "me" instead of "my marriage." Don't be in a hurry. I've seen many people healed after following these instructions. Repeat these prayers several times, believing in your heart that you are no longer a slave to Satan.

Heavenly Father, I sincerely repent of all involvement that may have caused a spirit of witchcraft, generational curses, or a stronghold to invade and influence my life. I pray for Your forgiveness. I am sorry for the hurt and pain I may have caused others through my actions. Father, I also want to forgive those who have harmed and tormented me. Today I make a decision to turn my life over to You and to walk in God's love. In the name of Jesus, amen!

Father, in the name of Jesus, I break all curses of witchcraft, abuse, and perversion over my flesh, and I surrender totally to You. I break all curses against my family in the name of

Jesus. I break all curses and any covenant made against [me/ my marriage], in the name of Jesus. I plead the blood of Jesus. I thank You, Father God, because Your Word declares that You will deliver me from every evil work and preserve me for Your heavenly kingdom. To Him be glory forever and ever [2 Tim. 4:18]. Amen!

Father God, Your Word declares that whatever I bind on the earth will be bound in heaven, and whatever I loose on the earth, will be loosed in heaven. I now bind all evil spirits attached to curses and covenants affecting my life, my family, and my marriage. I loose myself and my family from all inherited strongholds, sickness, disease, and addictions. I loose the peace and healing power of God to invade my life and heal my body, in the name of Jesus, amen!

Place your hands on your head and navel and pray:

Holy Spirit, I thank You for the miracle of deliverance from all curses and strongholds in my life. Holy Spirit, root out and destroy everything in me that is not of You, from the top of my head to the soles of my feet, in Jesus's name, amen!

Dear Holy Spirit, cleanse my heart, my womb, and every organ in my body.

Concentrate and stay focused until you experience God's peace invading your spirit, soul, and body.

Now say this prayer:

Father God, I thank You for the blood of Jesus indwelling my body right now. Lord Jesus, thank You for sacrificing Your life and shedding Your blood so that I could be redeemed from all sin, iniquities, and all curses and strongholds of the enemy.

Now make this declaration with great boldness:

> *In the name of Jesus Christ, I command all evil spirits to leave me now. I loose myself from all control and bondage of the enemy, in Jesus's name. I loose myself from all soul ties and evil strategies of the enemy. I renounce Satan and confess my allegiance to the Lord Jesus Christ. No weapon formed against me shall prosper, in Jesus's name, amen!*

Now get up and praise the Lord, thank Him, and rejoice in your freedom.

This next instruction is important. Ask the Holy Spirit to indwell you and fill you with His Spirit. Ask for a fresh anointing over your life. Praise the Lord again.

> *Lord Jesus, surround me with Your protection and baptize me with the Holy Spirit and fire. Cover me with the blood of Jesus and surround me with Your mighty warrior angels. I thank You and praise Your holy name.*

> John answered, saying to all, "I indeed baptize you with water; but One mightier than I is coming, whose sandal strap I am not worthy to loose. He will baptize you with the Holy Spirit and fire."

> —LUKE 3:16

> *Father, I sincerely want to thank You for opening my spiritual eyes to see that the thief only comes to steal, and to kill, and to destroy. But You, my Father, have come that I may have life, and that I may have it more abundantly* [John 10:10].

Rebuke a harassing spirit firmly.

> *In the name of Jesus, I rebuke the devil from trespassing in my life. There is no truth in you. I bind every assignment of*

the enemy against my family and me. And I loose the peace of God into my life.

Father God, I sincerely thank You for blessing me with wisdom, knowledge, and understanding.

You are of your father the devil, and the desires of your father you want to do. He was a murderer from the beginning, and does not stand in the truth, because there is no truth in him. When he speaks a lie, he speaks from his own resources, for he is a liar and the father of it.

—JOHN 8:44

Father, I will stand fast in the liberty by which Christ has made us free. I refuse to be entangled again with a yoke of bondage [Gal. 5:1].

CHAPTER THREE

ACTIONS THAT PRODUCE MIRACLES AND HEALING

The wicked flee when no one pursues,
But the righteous are bold as a lion.

—PROVERBS 28:1

HEALING AND MIRACLES are supernatural acts of God. Our involvement is necessary. Our faith must take *action*, and we must believe that God will do His part.

THE RIGHTEOUS ARE BOLD AS A LION

+ David went after the lion and the bear attacking his sheep—God gave him the strength and fearlessness to deliver the lamb and kill the lion.
+ Joshua and his men marched around the walls of Jericho—God tore them down.
+ Elijah built an altar and prayed for fire—God consumed the altar with fire.
+ A widow obeyed the prophet and gathered all the empty containers she could find—God supplied and multiplied all the oil she needed.
+ Captain Naaman had leprosy and was told to dip seven times in a dirty river—God stretched out His hand and healed him.
+ Noah built the ark—God flooded the earth and saved him and his family.

- The woman with the issue of blood pushed her way through the crowd to touch Jesus—she was instantly healed.
- Moses stretched out the rod—God parted the sea.
- David put a stone in a slingshot, aimed it at the giant— God killed him instantly.
- One day after many years of hating my father, I took action and cried out to God to forgive him—God instantly healed my soul.
- Recently I surrendered totally to God, stopped begging Him for healing and instead started thanking and praising Him—God stretched forth His hand and healed me!

No matter how much Word we know, without faith and action a healing or a miracle will not take place.

A *healing* is a gradual recovery or a restoration to health. It's when a person gets cured, whether by taking prescribed medicine, homeopathic or therapeutic remedies, surgery, making nutritional changes, confessing God's Word and specific healing scriptures and prayers, or a combination of the above. A restorative healing takes place where the person recaptures and regains their vigor and well-being.

The thesaurus describes a *miracle* as: wonder, phenomenon, surprise, marvel. All these words can describe the miraculous. *Miracle* is defined as, "An extraordinary event manifesting divine intervention in human affairs."[1] Divine intervention is necessary for a miracle to occur.

Miracles are signs from God. Miracles transmit messages. Precisely because they are unusual or unprecedented according to the empirical and scientific laws of nature, miracles evoke awe and wonder. Miracles can shock us out of our complacency. They might even awaken us from our utilitarian slumbers. Miracles can inspire, or teach, or cause a re-consideration of the paths we have embarked upon, or even convert us. Sometimes, a miraculous event coincides with the object of a specific petitional prayer. Often, miracles involve events of physical healing. But the critical question for people of faith is always, what is God communicating through this event?[2]

When a person has done everything he or she can and exhausted all human avenues of intervention, and receive a healing from a deadly incurable cancer, we can honestly say this is definitely a miracle from God! When something happens, such as an accident, and you know you should have died but you survived, I believe this also is a miracle of divine intervention. When you are held up at gunpoint and the attacker releases you, God's mercy has miraculously intervened. When Jesus ordered demons to come out of an individual, and they obeyed and the person was healed and normal again, I consider this a supernatural miracle. When a sinner comes to Christ and his life is transferred from the kingdom of darkness into the kingdom of light—this too is a miraculous supernatural act of God. When a person is set free from generational curses and his life is transformed by the Word of God, a miraculous event has taken place.

Both a healing and a miracle require divine intervention or involvement. Our *active* faith and God's power to heal are the combination necessary to receive a healing or a miracle.

BOLD FAITH AND A FEARLESS ATTITUDE

My grandmother was known as a bold lioness in the spirit realm. She prayed with authority and fearless boldness for the sick and bound. One day my sister-in-law called her desperately because her six-year-old son was having one asthma attack after another, leaving the child limp and emaciated. Every medical therapy possible had been ineffective. The child was despondent and unable to sleep peacefully.

It was early morning when my grandmother arrived at the boy's home. When the door was opened, she didn't greet anyone or ask where the child was staying. Without one word she mechanically, like a robot soldier, headed upstairs directly into the child's room. She had never entered the home before, nor was she informed of the child's room. Upon entering the steamy room, she found the child fighting for his breath, unable to control the hacking cough. Immediately she gave a direct fearless command: "Spirit of infirmity, go from this child, right now, never to come back, in the name of Jesus!" That was it! No yelling, shaking, anointing with oil, pleading with God, or long lengthy prayer, but a direct command in the name of Jesus. The child was instantly healed. A total transformation took place at that very instant.

He grew up from a frail, thin, and sickly child to a robust and healthy young man, never having a recurrent incidence of asthma. I was a young adolescent myself, but I remember this vividly. Today I visit with this young man, who is now married and with grown children, and we still reminisce about this wonderful supernatural healing and many other great divine interventions that God has done in our family.

What price did my grandmother pay to be able to command such power with God? I believe it was her obedience and dependence on God's Word. Not only was she knowledgeable of her position in Christ and what the Bible says about our authority in the name of Jesus, but she also learned to develop fearlessness and to act with bold audacity against the devil. She knew the power of Christ Jesus in her was greater than the power of the enemy and that Satan has already been defeated on the cross of Calvary. Every home she entered every day was never the same after she left. Sickness, fever, demons, and confusion had to leave when Grandma spoke the Word.

Casting out fear

Jesus taught us to lay hands on the sick. We can't allow fear to stop us from obeying this command (Mark 16:18). We must develop a fearless attitude when we pray for healing miracles. Doubt has to be dragged away like a corpse. As we develop a positive attitude and a bold faith language, we will start to see the miraculous.

Fear must be cast out of our hearts. Many people never receive because of feelings of inferiority and timidity. Fear and faith cannot operate at the same time. We must live in the Spirit with a consciousness that our active faith is what moves the hand of God. Our fears will be defeated when our soul is restored. Satan will not be able to confuse or stop us from obeying God's Word. Faith to receive healing comes through the Word of God.

THE ROLE OF INTENSE PRAYER IN HEALING

Our prayer time should not be a time to beg God for something, but it should express our faith that He is able to perform His Word. When we pray God's Word, our hope becomes faith. The prayer of faith will release our faith into *action* and produce powerful results and fulfillment.

The strongest enemy of our faith is an unrenewed mind, because it produces unbelief. The prayer of faith is a very vital part of the healing process. Agreement with God's Word will cause great mountains of sickness and problems to be moved.

Enter prayer with God's Word in your mouth. Take up your weapon of the sword of the Spirit to defeat Satan. Effective fervent prayers of agreement with God's Word will minister healing to your body and to the sick. Real faith is specific; unclear and doubtful prayers can't get the job done. For miracles to happen, we must not doubt in our hearts but remain fully focused and persuaded that what God has promised, He is able to perform (Rom. 4:20–21). Our desire for a miracle must be so intense that we believe in our spirits it is already done (Mark 11:24).

Science has proven that, like fingerprints, every human voice has what is called a *print*. Your *voiceprint*, like your fingerprint, is different from all other voices. Father God knows your voice and waits to hear it when you praise Him every day. When you believe that God is hearing you, you will pray with faith and expectancy (James 5:16; Eph. 6:17–18).

I remember that for many years I had a vision of reaching millions with the message God has placed in my heart of, "Satan, you can't have my children, my marriage, my miracle, my inheritance, and my body." I saw this vision in my mind, and I praised God for its timing and fulfill-ment. In the meantime I prepared and kept writing and teaching every-where I was invited. One day the doors opened through my first book, *Satan, You Can't Have My Children*, published by Charisma House. My intense prayers, persistence, and preparation have produced a har-vest. Many people are receiving encouragement, hope, and instruction to stand and resist the devil. Your powerful prayers will move moun-tains. The miracle is in your mouth!

HEALING FROM INHERITED AND INCURABLE DISEASES

Although I am enjoying forty-one good years of marriage, I have also been actively contending with a debilitating disease for seventeen years—a disease without a medical cure and for which I am taking medication. Many times I have felt the urge to give up, retire from min-istry and writing, and lead a passive life. In retrospect I can see how the enemy would have loved for me to give up, become bitter, and adapt myself to a life of complaining and instability.

Instead I have chosen to believe and apply God's Word to my mind and body. My daily practice includes thanking God for healing and declaring that I am healed by faith even though I do not see a complete manifestation. My quest for healing has taken me to many physicians and different therapies. Pain in my body has become a frequent unwel-come companion, which I put under subjection with prayer and confes-sion every night and morning. Do I complain, mumble, and grumble all the time? Please ask my husband and my daughters. They will tell you that I barely ever complain. They know I'm hurting when they see me reach for the pain medication. I have tremendous peace and know that Jesus is the healer whether I receive my total healing or not. My life has become an open testimony to many people of God's sustaining power.

When I get in front of an audience to speak, the Holy Spirit sustains me and enables me to deliver without pain or discomfort. I feel ener-gized. I travel all the time, sometimes across continents, and God has been faithful to me. I remember a few weeks ago dashing as quickly as

I could from one terminal to the other in the airport to make a connection. At first I thought I would succumb from the pain and not be able to make it on time, but as I hopped from one moving belt to the next I started confessing a scripture over and over: "I can do all things through Christ who strengthens me" (Phil. 4:13). I was exhilarated and flushed when I arrived at the gate without one bit of pain in my body. The supernatural power of God's Word just took over as I confessed and believed that I could run and leap and not be wearied or consumed. "For by You I can run against a troop, by my God I can leap over a wall" (Ps. 18:29).[3]

My bold confession

Several months ago when I started writing this book on the miraculous power of God to heal, I made a daring statement to my heavenly Father:

> My Abba Father, I believe that as I write this book about
> Your miraculous power to heal and transform people's lives,
> I will receive my miracle of healing, for nothing is impossible for You!

I started boldly acting on my faith in a new dimension. I am so excited to announce that my last exam a few weeks ago was the most wonderful report I've received in eighteen years. Everything was normal! Nothing was negative! Praise God! My doctor refuses to acknowledge a miracle occurred but claims that I've gone into a sudden remission, but I choose to believe that my God has miraculously healed me of what the doctors claim is an incurable disease. For the first time in a long time my fingers don't ache as I type and my knees don't hurt as I sit for hours.

The doctor who took care of me for many years kept telling me that I needed to increase the cortisone and add different medications, which I tried on different occasions, but they only made my situation worse. He had lost an adult daughter to the same illness and was adamant that I should follow his advice. Though I don't recommend to anyone that they follow my example of not taking all the medications recommended in a similar situation, I do recommend that you follow my advice at the end of this chapter, declaring and confessing God's Word to build up your faith for a miracle of healing. Your confession of God's Word is not what will heal you, but it will build up your faith. Your faith and obedience in action will dethrone all of Satan's attacks against you. It doesn't matter what illness you may be dealing with or if you're battling cancer or an incurable disease; nothing is too impossible for my God! Jesus said:

> The things which are impossible with men are possible with God.
>
> —LUKE 18:27

I like to take God's Word literally and apply it to all circumstances—*especially the ones an expert says and believes are impossibilities to overcome.* I am so excited and motivated to really get this message across to the millions suffering in silence. I am still basking in my miracle! I am able to sleep in whatever position I now want. I am able to run up and down the stairs. I am able to type really fast. Wow! What an awesome and miraculous God we serve! What are you waiting for? Read this book several times. Mark it up, and add your own scriptures and prayers. Don't forget your spiritual sacrifices at the end of this chapter. Those were the highlights of my miracle.

INDISPENSABLE: THE BLOOD OF JESUS AND THE HELP OF THE HOLY SPIRIT

After doing all these things I'm recommending to you, I woke up healed! Whether you believe all this stuff or not, it really works. The blood of Jesus is the balm, the force, the power, and the means by which the Bible says you have already been healed. Praise God. The Holy Spirit will be your teacher and will reveal the Word of God to you. You cannot leave these two out of the equation. You might as well give up if you hold back from taking the whole package that God has granted and paid a great price for us to enjoy. I am writing in simple English for you to understand this message. Many of you do understand and could probably write this in a more beautiful style than I am, but God is using me at this precise moment to reveal and present this message clearly to so many countless millions of wounded and afflicted people who are unaware of the precious wonderful gift that God has bestowed to us—Jesus Christ, our healer and Redeemer!

I am here in writing to open your spiritual eyes to understand the supernatural dimension you're involved in, whether you discern it or not. I want to interrupt your thinking to see new visions, new understanding and capacity, to know God's greatness, and to help you receive your healing and soul transformation.

The Bible proclaims that we are a royal priesthood. Healing and restoration belong to God's children. When the economy is down, our economy should be up. When the storms rock your boat, Jesus should be right there with you to still the storms. When the doctors say your diagnosis is positive and incurable, God's Word says, "NO! Trust Me! Ask Me to move the mountain!" Have faith in God!

Grow your mustard seed

The ministry my husband and I do requires much travel and long hours of teaching and preparation. Our travels have taken us to many cities and countries around the world. As I write at this moment, I'm sitting on a plane from Paris to Dallas, Texas, after spending ten days in Florence, Italy, doing several family conferences. God in His mercy has met all my expectations. You see, I believe that expectation is hope, anticipation, belief, eagerness, and looking forward to something. Expectation is a quality necessary to overcome adverse circumstances. My expectation is that God will perform His Word in your body as He has done in my body and in my life. I believe that as I walk in faith and obedience, the mustard seed of faith the Bible declares we can possess begins to get bigger and bigger, and I am able to see the miraculous evolve before my very eyes.

The tiny mustard seed grows into a large tree with huge branches and leaves. The birds enjoy roosting and nesting in its branches. So it is with a person who develops his faith—it spiritually grows into a large fruitful tree. People will gravitate and come to you for help and ministry. As you develop and grow your faith, you will learn to believe God for the impossible. You will see and experience the miraculous divine intervention of almighty God in your own life.

> For truly I say to you, if you have faith [that is living] like a grain of mustard seed, you can say to this mountain, Move from here to yonder place, and it will move; and nothing will be impossible to you.
>
> —MATTHEW 17:20, AMP

The Bible says that we all have been allotted a measure of faith (Rom. 12:3). Even a tiny bit of faith the size of a mustard seed can produce your healing! I dare you to start putting your faith into action and believing God for miracles, healing, and restoration of your soul.

God wants to heal His people and protect them from accidents and all the strategies of Satan. Don't allow your feelings to overpower your faith. If God's Word says that by the stripes of Jesus we are healed, then agree with it. Declare the scriptures and prayers at the end of this chapter to build up your faith. Start closing every door in your life that has given the devil permission to harass your life with sickness and problems.

WHY ARE SO MANY CHRISTIANS SICK AND OPPRESSED?

Sickness and disease touch almost every family on the earth. Many sick people are spending all their substance on remedies, diets, medications, and doctors but are becoming worse each day. I believe the reason why more Christians do not receive their healing is because of lack of knowledge and obedience. They just don't understand or know what the Word of God says about what Jesus's sacrifice on the cross of Calvary purchased for them. Other Christians simply do not know how to pray and worship God. Others have a hard time obeying God's principles for divine healing. It is estimated that at least 80 percent of people in America are Christians. Yet the percentage of sick people is about the same as non-Christians who don't believe in Jesus our healer.

I frequently hear sick people say, "I'm not sure if it is God's will to heal me....If only I knew. Maybe I'm supposed to be sick to keep me humble or build up my faith." When God's Word promises healing in the new covenant, we should not be asking or saying, "If it be Your will." This implies a lack of faith.

Doubt and unbelief are deadly—they kill your faith, and without faith you will never obtain the promises that are legally yours. Be watchful over your heart and diligently guard what you allow to come into your life. Each person you allow into your life will plant seeds, just as the Pharisees did in the lives of the disciples. If Satan can cause a seed of doubt and unbelief to be planted in your life, he is on his way to stealing your faith. If the enemy can steal your faith, he can steal everything in your life and everything God has predestined for you. A lifestyle of doubt says to God that He is a liar and cannot be trusted. Doubt and unbelief will prevent you from obtaining the prosperity that God declares is yours. Choose not to fall into the trap of the enemy, and choose to believe God, *no matter what*. He is your healer and deliverer (Matt. 21:21; 13:58).

YOUR HEALING IS GUARANTEED!

Jesus Christ gave His life as a sacrifice. Isaiah 53 assures us that Christ took upon Himself all our grief, sorrows, pain, affliction, transgressions, iniquities, and all our sins. By His scourging, by His wounds, and by His death and resurrection we are healed. Everything in God's kingdom you receive by faith. Without faith you can't receive. You receive healing the same way you receive salvation. You confess it and believe it in your heart. It's our divine born-again birthright (inheritance, entitlement, legacy, and privilege). Don't settle for less than God's best for you.

What is the thing you've been battling for so long? You have a choice to make, to either stay in the same situation, or decide to turn your situation over to God and dare to believe Him for a miraculous healing and transformation. It's your faith in action that will start moving out the evil squatters. It's your move.

Regardless of your circumstances, Abba Father is ready to meet you exactly where you are right now. All God needs is your faith to believe that He is willing to heal you. *Faith is trust.* When you trust someone, you love and respect the person. Father God is the same way with us. He loves us unconditionally. *When we surrender to His love and obey His Word, He produces.* His gifts are extremely valuable and priceless.

You don't have to make sacrifices and quote scriptures day and night. The reason I'm listing the scriptures and declarations at the end of each chapter is because they will build up your faith and teach you how to stay in contact and relationship with your healer and Savior. There is something unique about declaring God's Word. It puts angels on the alert and causes evil spirits to flee. Evil spirits cannot trespass when our spiritual borders are reinforced with prayers and the Word of God. Really think about this. It is life transforming. When you deposit God's Word into your heart and mind, it becomes a lifeline and health to all your body. I quote and take literally Proverbs 4:20–22 every day because I believe God is the Word and He is *life*!

Your prayers and declarations of God's Word are not to move the hand of God on your behalf but to strengthen your inner man and build up your faith. God is moved by compassion and love. All we have to do is surrender to His will, obey His Word, and love one another.

Do we have to make sacrifices to receive healing?

Please don't skip this powerful section. The only sacrifices mentioned in the New Testament are the *sacrifices of praise and thanksgiving and the sacrifice of joy.* I don't know about you, but this was liberating news for me. I don't have to sacrifice by begging, confessing, memorizing prayers and scriptures, fasting, going to all the church services, keeping a serious face all the time, or abstaining from certain things. I don't have to perform sacrifices by killing an animal every day, as Job did every day for each one of his family members (Job 1). God loves us, and He loves our worship and praise and our thanksgiving and joy.

To sacrifice is to offer something to God. To *sacrifice* means, "to give up something of value, to make an offering, to surrender, to kill, to give up, to dedicate, consecrate, devote, and to benefit." A sacrifice will cost you time, focus, killing the flesh, surrendering your will for a higher cause. The benefit we receive can never be calculated. Every sacrifice we make is compensated and backed up by all of God's promises and treasures.

THE SACRIFICES OF PRAISE, THANKSGIVING, AND JOY

When we bring our sacrifices of *praise, thanksgiving, and joy* to God, we are telling Him that we wish to die to our own desires and knowledge, and we desire to love and trust Him completely.

The sacrifices of praise and thanksgiving

It is in the holy atmosphere of praise and worship that healing, miracles, and transformation of the soul begins to manifest, and God's glory starts cleansing and changing our carnal nature into the nature and character of Christ. We are literally praying with our heart, soul, and spirit. The result is always an impartation of God's infinite blessings, wisdom, knowledge, and understanding. When you truly understand this truth, you will begin to regain and restore all that Satan has stolen from you. Demons cannot resist the praise of the children of God. *Wow!* I'm a believer! I'm enjoying every moment of my life.

When you feel discouraged and a spirit of confusion tries to invade your thinking, if you begin to offer a sacrifice of praise and thanksgiving, you will find that the peace of God will cover you as a shield of protection and the angel of the Lord will encamp all around you and deliver you (Ps. 34:7). I remember God's protection during a holdup and how I had offered a *sacrifice of praise and thanksgiving* before we left the hotel room.

Being the victim of a holdup is a bewildering experience. Numbness seems to paralyze the person and make him or her hostage to the predator. Two years ago I was in Mexico with my husband waiting at a stoplight, when suddenly the side door of our van was abruptly opened and a gunman thrust a gun into the driver's face demanding that he give him his jewels and cash. His eyes quickly darted to the backseat where my husband and I were seated. He flashed the gun at us also demanding that we strip of our jewels and cash. The light was still red, and he wanted us to quickly obey his commands before that light turned green. All I remember in that quick minute was to say a prayer under my breath, "Satan, the blood of Jesus is against you. I command this man's finger to freeze so that he can't pull the trigger. Thank You, Father." He managed to get away with two watches, and though he demanded that I take off my jewels, I was miraculously unable to take off my diamond earrings and wedding rings. The light changed, and the assailant was gone. Our lives were protected by divine intervention. We were told that many have died in the middle of traffic in similar situations. I immediately realized that on that same morning I had offered a sacrifice of praise and thanksgiving and declared, "No weapon formed against us shall prosper." God protects His children from all manner of situations, attacks, and accidents. We should never leave the house without offering a *sacrifice of praise and thanksgiving*. We cannot be afraid to pray with boldness, even if our knees are shaking. Our actions will determine the outcome of every situation.

The sacrifice of joy

Joy means, "delight, pleasure, enjoyment, bliss, ecstasy, elation, happiness, joyfulness, thrill, wonder, triumph, and jubilation." The *sacrifice of joy* is the most difficult sacrifice to offer to God. If you're depressed and oppressed by demons, you may frown at the word *joy*. You may find it easier to praise God and offer thanksgiving. But when we're sad and afflicted, going through storms and difficulties in life, or when sickness afflicts our bodies, then it becomes a real *sacrifice* to lift our voices and offer a *sacrifice of joy*. But let me share a secret with you.

The Bible says that *the joy of the Lord is our strength* (Neh. 8:10). Strength is power. Strength is emotional toughness and resistance. Strength is defensive ability. Strength is effectiveness to succeed and achieve. Strength makes you progressively better. We offer this type of sacrifice singing melodies, dancing, reciting psalms, and declaring aloud those things that are not as though they are, smiling, laughing, clapping our hands, and rejoicing in what the Lord says about us.

My precious mother, who is eighty-three years old and bedridden, may not be able to sit or walk or do many of the things she was so accustomed to doing, but you would be amazed to see her display of praise, thanksgiving, and joy. Her inner man is strong and confident. Her mind doesn't suffer from Alzheimer's disease. She can't hear very well, but when you enter her room, her hands are raised up to heaven in a sacrifice of joy. Everyone who visits her receives a big smile, a blessing, an encouraging word, and songs from years gone by.

Every morning I feel God's goodness invade my atmosphere. My home is peaceful. Healing greets every visitor. God is a merciful Father and desires to bless you with healing and wholeness. It is by His grace (kindness, blessing, mercy, generosity, divine favor) that we receive all good things. Grace is a gift. God desires our love. He wants to passionately love us. The closer we draw to the Holy Spirit, the more we learn to love God with all our heart. Father God wants to shower us with an outpouring of His miraculous healing and blessings.

SCRIPTURES AND PRAYERS TO BUILD UP
YOUR FAITH AND RECEIVE HEALING

Sacrifice of praise and worship

Heavenly Father, I enter Your courts with praise and adoration, for You alone are holy and worthy to be praised. I lift up my hands in surrender to You, and I exalt and glorify Your name. I will praise You, Lord, for Your mercy endures forever. My heart draws near to You seeking to worship You in spirit and truth. Your Word declares in 1 Peter 2:5 that we are a royal priesthood to offer up spiritual sacrifices acceptable to God through Jesus Christ. I glorify, honor, and magnify Your holy name [John 4:23–24].

Therefore by Him let us continually offer the sacrifice of praise to God, that is, the fruit of our lips, giving thanks to His name.

—HEBREWS 13:15

Sacrifice of thanksgiving

My Lord and Savior, I thank You for giving me life and for breathing Your Spirit into my spirit. Thank You for saving me and transforming my life. Thank You for directing my steps each day. Thank You because I am justified and accepted in Christ Jesus. Thank You for Your provision and protection each day. Thank You for renewing my mind as I study Your Word. Thank You for blessing my family and keeping us from all evil. Thank You for keeping me from all temptations and wrong decisions. Thank You for healing my body and strengthening my bones. Thank You for the Spirit of wisdom and revelation.

Keep adding your thanksgiving to this prayer. If you need to practice, start reciting some of the psalms of praise and thanksgiving.

Lord, I will sacrifice the sacrifices of thanksgiving, and declare Your works with rejoicing [Ps. 107:22].

Lord, I will be anxious for nothing, but in everything by prayer and supplication, with thanksgiving, I will let my requests be made known to You [Phil. 4:6].

I will offer to You the sacrifice of thanksgiving, and will call upon the name of the LORD.

—PSALM 116:17

I will praise the LORD according to His righteousness, and I will sing praise to the name of the LORD Most High.

—PSALM 7:17

Sacrifice of joy

My Lord, I offer to You a sacrifice of joy. I will sing praises to the Lord, for You are my exceeding joy, my God, and my King. I rejoice that I belong to You. I rejoice that Christ died for us for the joy of obtaining the prize before Him, enduring the cross so that we could be delivered from the kingdom of darkness and restored to the kingdom of light. I too offer a sacrifice of joy, enduring all hardships for the joy of eternal life. The joy of the Lord is my strength [Heb. 12:2; Neh. 8:10].

And now I will lift up my head above my enemies all around me, and I will offer sacrifices of joy to You my Lord. I will sing, yes, I will sing praises to the Lord [Ps. 27:6].

Lord, I bring my praises to the altar of God, to God my exceeding joy. I will always praise You, O God, my God [Ps. 43:4].

My King, I praise Your name with songs of joy and with dancing. I rejoice because You alone can fill my heart with gladness [Ps. 149:3].

Prayers to receive healing

Father, I believe that as I pay attention to Your Word and I meditate on it and keep Your sayings in my heart, Your words become life and health to all my body. I thank You, Father, for this promise. I apply this truth as medicine and declare that I am healed and whole, in Jesus's name!

My son, give attention to my words; incline your ear to my sayings. Do not let them depart from your eyes; keep them in the midst of your heart; for they are life to those who find them, and health to all their flesh.

—PROVERBS 4:20–22

I declare that the Spirit of God who raised Jesus from the dead dwells in me, cleansing every area of my body attacked by infirmity. I rebuke all sickness, disease, pestilence, and every noisome and foul thing attached to my body. I loose myself from your grip right now in the name of Jesus [Rom. 8:11; Ps. 91:3].

Father, I believe that by the stripes of Jesus I am healed. I loose myself from every spirit of infirmity that attacks my body, in the name of Jesus [Isa. 53:5].

Pain, inflammation, swelling, migraines, arthritis, and fibromyalgia

I cast out every spirit of pain, inflammation, swelling, migraines, arthritis, and fibromyalgia caused by inheritance, accidents, or generational curses. I apply the blood of Jesus to my body and declare that I am healed! I take up the shield of faith, and in Jesus's name I quench all the fiery darts of the wicked one [Eph. 6:16].

Weakness, viruses

Father, I believe that Christ Himself took our infirmities [illnesses, frailties, disabilities, and lack of strength] and bore our sicknesses [diseases, viruses, infections, and all known and unknown illnesses], and I decree that the blood of Jesus cleanses and makes me whole [Matt. 8:17].

In the name of Jesus, no evil disease will cling to me. I break the power of the evil one from tormenting my body [Ps. 41:8].

Heart disease

I curse the root of all heart disease. I break its power over me and my children and their children. I declare that I have a sound heart and long life, in Jesus's name [Prov. 14:30].

Father, Your Word says that those who seek the Lord shall not lack any good thing. I thank You for healing my body [Ps. 34:10].

Cancer, fever, afflictions, distress, diseases, disorders, suffering

Father, Your Word declares that many are the afflictions of Your people, but the Lord delivers them out of them all. Thank You for delivering me out of this affliction. I curse the root of cancer, fever, and pestilence. I drive out these tormenting spirits of infirmity in the name of Jesus! You have no authority over my body. I've been redeemed from the curse of sickness and disease! I command every plant that my heavenly Father has not planted to be uprooted, in the name of Jesus [Ps. 34:19; Hab. 3:5; Matt. 15:13].

Diabetes, arthritis, pain in the knees, legs, hands, boils, ulcers

> *Father God, I believe that through Christ we have been redeemed from the curse of the law and all the curses listed in Deuteronomy. In the name of Jesus, I break the power of all infirmity causing diabetes, arthritis, and pain in my knees, legs, hands, and severe boils and ulcers, which refuse to be healed, and from the soles of my feet to the top of my head, I command my body to be made whole, in the name of Jesus* [Gal. 3:13–14; Deut. 28:35; Isa. 35:3; Heb. 12:12–13].

> *Father, Your Word declares that everyone who asks, receives, and he who seeks, finds, and to him who knocks it will be opened. I am seeking Your face and asking in faith. Thank You for Your healing power driving all sickness and disease out of my body* [Matt. 7:8].

Pestilence (epidemic, plague, virus, pandemic, deadly disease, bubonic plague)

> *Father, Your Word declares that You will surely deliver us from the snare of the fowler and from the perilous pestilence. I believe Your Word. In the name of Jesus, I resist the devil, and he must flee from me. I curse all roots of disease and pestilence from attacking my body and my loved ones. I plead the blood of Jesus and decree that greater is Christ in me. No weapon formed against me shall prosper, in the name of Jesus* [Ps. 91:3, 6; James 4:7; Isa. 54:17].

Blood and bones (blood pressure, leukemia, diabetes, anemia, osteoporosis)

> *Father, Your Word declares that by the stripes of Jesus I am healed and that if I fear the Lord and depart from evil, it shall be health to my flesh and strength to my bones. I believe that*

I am the temple of God and that the Spirit of God dwells in me. I thank You, Father, for cleansing my blood and restoring my weak bones. Your Word declares that You keep my bones and not one of them is broken. I believe that Your Word penetrates my joints and marrow and I walk in divine health. In the name of Jesus, I curse the root of sickness and disease in my blood and my joints and marrow. I speak wholeness to my entire body. I curse the root of all inherited and generational disease in my family and bloodline. In Jesus's name and by the power of His blood, I declare that I am healed [Prov. 3:5–8; Heb. 4:12; Joel 3:21; 1 Cor. 3:16; Ps. 6:2; 34:20; Isa. 58:11].

Nervous conditions

Father, thank You because You are my refuge and strength and my help when I'm in trouble. You are faithful, and You promise to establish me and keep me from all evil. I declare that You are my confidence, and You will keep my foot from being caught. Father, I remind You of Your Word to cast my cares upon the Lord and You shall sustain me. I need help. I thank You for giving me the strength to overcome the power of the enemy. I now take authority over every plan and strategy of the enemy against my life. In Jesus's name, I rebuke the devil, and he must flee from me. I bind all demonic spirits attacking my nervous system, and I loose the peace of God into my life right now [Ps. 46:1; 2 Thess. 3:3; Prov. 3:26; Ps. 55:22].

Healing prayer to restore the immune system, heal tiredness, and joint pain

I command the immune system to be restored. I command it to be effective in stopping diseases, germs, and viruses from inflicting this body, in Jesus's name. I command all of the electrical and magnetic frequencies in this body to return to normal harmony and balance. I command all the prions to completely dissolve and be discarded from the body. I command healing to every cell affected by these prions, in Jesus's name.[4]

Prayer of agreement to receive healing

When the prayer of agreement is made according to Matthew 18:18–20, it will cover every condition and situation that needs divine intervention.

> Assuredly, I say to you, whatever you bind on earth will be bound in heaven, and whatever you loose on earth will be loosed in heaven. Again I say to you that if two of you agree on earth concerning anything that they ask, it will be done for them by My Father in heaven. For where two or three are gathered together in My name, I am there in the midst of them.
>
> —MATTHEW 18:18–20

Perhaps I have not mentioned your ailment in this section. It doesn't matter what your sickness, disease, or disorder may be, Christ Jesus is ready to heal you. Have you read this section carefully? Have you surrendered your heart to God? Have you cleansed yourself of all evil influences? Have you prepared your heart to receive? When you're ready, you may pray the prayer of agreement to receive healing. I have already asked the Holy Spirit to intervene on your behalf. Believe in your heart that your prayer is powerful and that God will heal and restore you. You may say this prayer several times until you feel confident that you're yielding with your whole heart.

PRAYER OF AGREEMENT

Father God, I come boldly into Your presence joining in a prayer of agreement with Iris Delgado [or your prayer partner], *bringing to Your remembrance Isaiah 53:5 and 1 Peter 2:24: But He was wounded for our transgressions, He was bruised for our iniquities; the chastisement for our peace*

was upon Him, and by His stripes we are healed. Father, we
believe and come into agreement that Christ Jesus already paid
the price for my healing and restoration.

Father, Your Word declares that the prayer of faith shall
save the sick, and the Lord shall raise him up, and if he has
committed sins, he will be forgiven [James 5:15]. You also
promise in Exodus 15:26 that You are the Lord who heals us.
I come against the afflictions and attacks of the enemy against
my body, and I speak restoration and wholeness into my body
right now in Jesus's name! By faith, I declare that I am healed!

In Jesus's name, I believe that I am healed. I believe that
I receive healing from [be specific: name the condition]
_____. *We establish this agreement in the*

name of Jesus, amen!

Perhaps you won't venture daring prayers against evil powers such
as "Oh, Lord, please strike my enemies and break their teeth." But
David prayed bold and specific prayers against his enemies. "Arise, O
LORD; save me, O my God! For You have struck all my enemies on
the cheekbone; You have broken the teeth of the ungodly" (Ps. 3:7).
Don't be afraid to be bold and specific. Satan is not afraid of you. You
shouldn't be afraid of him. The power of God in you is greater than the
power of the enemy. Your active faith and participation will tear down
the walls of the enemy.

The Word of God is medicine. When we pray and obey God's
Word, *it becomes life to those who find them and health to all their flesh*
(Prov. 4:20–22).

Testimony of the effects of a prayer of agreement

My husband and I have learned to pray in agreement concerning
important decisions and for divine protection over our family, ministry, and businesses. At one time we owned a jewelry store. All of our
employees were Christians, and every morning we prayed in agreement
for protection from all evil. A thief came in dressed in a long trench

coat and with his hands in his pockets. Immediately my husband, who was in the back and saw him come in, commanded all the employees in the back room to pray and intercede, while he walked to the front of the store. An employee was already asking the thief if he could be of help, at which he quickly demanded that the employee empty a specific showcase and place all the items in a bag he threw at him, while at the same time pointing a gun at his stomach. I remember my specific prayer, "My Father, thank You for protection. Stay the hand of the enemy. Satan, I bind your plan, and I bind this man from harming anyone here, in Jesus's name, amen."

One of our armed employees saw the gun and immediately aimed at the robber, telling him to drop his gun, but instead the thief swung around, aiming at the employee with his gun. Within seconds the robber was running out of the store with a gunshot to his head, dropping outside the door, instantly dead. When the police arrived, they congratulated our staff for a job well done. The assailant was an ex-con with a long track record of assaults and had come from another jewelry store in town where a round of gunshots had completely missed him.

I believe God's angels were in our store supervising everything. Our warfare prayers of agreement instantly put God's warrior angels to work. "He who dwells in the secret place of the Most High shall abide under the shadow of the Almighty" (Ps. 91:1). God's shadow is always over His children who dwell in His presence. If our actions had been different, displaying fear and panic, our situation could have been much different. Your specific powerful prayers will accomplish exactly what you command them to do. We were all in agreement. God says, "You do, and I will do. You obey, and I will bless you. You send the Word, and I will perform it. You believe in faith, and I will act."

CHAPTER FOUR

EXPECTING AND COMMANDING THE MIRACULOUS EVERY DAY

*He who dwells in the secret place of the Most High
shall remain stable and fixed under the shadow of the
Almighty [Whose power no foe can withstand].*

—PSALM 91:1, AMP

A FEW YEARS AGO I was coming out of a South Florida supermarket in a great hurry to get home. As I was walking briskly toward my car, fumbling for my car keys, I felt someone grab my purse, sending a shooting pain through my arm as the mugger pulled on my purse with all his might. My first instinct was to hold on to my purse and scream. It was broad daylight, and people watched helplessly, unable or unwilling to get involved. I remember crying out to God for help, realizing that the man was armed with a gun and my life was in danger. I quickly let go of the purse as I heard the man's voice say, "Let go, or I'll kill you!" Off he ran with my purse into a waiting car.

EQUIPPED AND FEARLESS—MIRACLES OF ANGELIC PROTECTION

All believers have angelic protection at their disposal. Other than swelling on my arm and hand, I was unharmed. I believe my life was spared at that moment by a miracle of God's supernatural intervention. My situation seemed unpredictable, and Satan had every intention to harm me. Talk about divine intervention! That morning I had changed purses and left my valuable jewelry pouch with my diamond wedding rings, as well as my credit cards, inside my closet. I really had no specific reason to change purses, except my hands were hurting and swollen, and my purse felt heavy. I opted for a smaller purse with bare necessities to make a quick grocery purchase.

The Spirit of God in me was already aware of the oncoming situation. The shadow of the Almighty was covering me as it covers every believer in Christ Jesus. I realize many people have an obsession with angels, but this is not about obsession. This is about what the Word says about God's mighty messenger angels; they are always ready to help and defend us from the attacks of the enemy.

> For He shall give His angels charge over you, to keep you in all your ways. In their hands they shall bear you up, lest you dash your foot against a stone.
>
> —Psalm 91:11–12

Apostle Ronald Short, our spiritual father, taught us that when doing spiritual warfare and ministering to people with torment, addictions, or sickness, a servant of God has to have a fearless attitude and disposition. There cannot be any wavering, doubt, unbelief, or hesitancy. Prayers must be bold, direct, specific, focused, and with expectancy for miracles to happen.

Maintaining a fervent prayer life is absolutely critical to strengthen your spirit, mind, and body and make you fearless against the enemy. Your relationship with the Holy Spirit for guidance and wisdom also depends on a fervent and powerful prayer habit. If you're lacking in this area, then you're already experiencing trouble and weaknesses. "The effective, fervent prayer of a righteous man avails much" (James 5:16).

My husband was involved in a car accident while on his way to a Christian TV program with the president of the network. Just as they were taking a deep turn on the highway, an eighteen-wheeler missed the turn and instead smashed against my husband's car and into a cement retainer wall. The vehicle was a small rental car that was instantly crushed on all sides. Both my husband and his companion walked out without a scratch or a headache—a supernatural divine intervention. Yes! This was a supernatural miracle, and God's messengers were quick to intervene on their behalf.

When we breathe in God's Word and it indwells our being, it controls and directs our thinking and actions. We become renewed, refreshed, satisfied, directed, purposeful, confident, and powerful! The following psalm is a powerful prayer that reminds us of God's undivided attention to His children. Memorize and personalize this prayer and pray it every day.

> Bless the LORD, O my soul; and all that is within me, bless His holy name! Bless the LORD, O my soul, and forget not all His benefits: who forgives all your iniquities, who heals all your diseases, who redeems your life from destruction, who crowns you with lovingkindness and tender mercies, who satisfies your mouth with good things, so that your youth is renewed like the eagle's.
>
> —PSALM 103:1–5

The miracle of protection from enemy attacks

While in Vietnam as a medic in the most dangerous years of the war, 1968–1969, my husband was surrounded by bullets and grenades flying across his head and all around him as he tended to the wounded and dragged many out of harm's way. Among his battalion he was one of the few who made it out alive—supernatural divine intervention. Praying parents and a congregation back home believed God and stood in the gap. This is proof of the effectiveness of intercession and united prayer. It is also proof of the power of our prayers and God's awesome mercy.

The miracle of protection from a car accident

As I wrote this book, my daughter was driving home from work on a beautiful clear afternoon. She was on the speakerphone with her cousin in Florida. Everything seemed normal, and traffic was flowing smoothly, when all of a sudden, she felt an unexpected violent jolt against the back of her vehicle. One moment she was sitting up minding her own business, and the next moment she heard and felt the crunching and metallic sounds that slammed her body into the steering wheel then backward, breaking her seat. In bewilderment she tried to raise her head to see what was happening, when in unbelief she saw her car being pushed out of control toward two other cars in front of her, which slammed into both sides of the front of her car.

As she wondered about her predicament, she realized she was alive and conscious. Within minutes a policemen came to assess the situation, and the first thing he told her was, "You are lucky today. Most people don't walk out of accidents like this one. You better put every penny the insurance gives you back into the same type of car, because this car saved your life."

My daughter then said, "This car did not save my life; my God saved my life!"

The police officer looked at her and said, "You must have a BIG God!"

Wow! We sure do! Miraculously my daughter was helped out of the car unharmed. Not one of her bones was broken, and not a drop of blood was shed.

The angel of the Lord was on assignment, for the Bible says, "The angel of the LORD encamps all around those who fear Him, and delivers them" (Ps. 34:7).

The driver of the eighteen-wheeler confessed that he was in another lane, but all of a sudden the driver in front of him stopped, and he was forced to make an instant decision of slamming his trailer full force into the stopped car in front of him, creating a multiple car pileup accident, or getting over to the next lane with less traffic but also knowing he would have to slam into the vehicle in front of him, which happened to be my daughter's. The force of the impact pushed her car forty feet into two cars in front of her, causing a four-car pile-up. All we can say is that God miraculously protected her life. X-rays, an MRI, and many other exams came out negative. Nothing was out of place. Small bruises on her arm were the only telltale signs of the shocking accident.

That morning I was up earlier than usual, lifting up my family in powerful prayers, expecting and commanding the miraculous and breaking all demonic assignments and evil interruptions. A hedge of protection was in place. When you form a habit of surrendering your life and your family to God each day, you place God's warrior angels on assignment. They are messengers that await instructions not only from God but also from God's children. (See Psalm 103:20; Acts 12:7.)

THE POWER OF THE HOLY SPIRIT

The Holy Spirit is the power in the believer to set the captives free. The Holy Spirit at work in you will play the greatest role of soul transformation and healing above any other method, sacrifice, therapy, or process of change you engage in. The disciples were filled with the Holy Spirit when Jesus breathed on them (John 20:22). They were able to pray for the sick and tormented people, and miracles were manifested.

The Holy Spirit resides inside every believer. Our body is the temple of the Holy Spirit. Peter told the beggar in Acts 3:6: "Silver and gold I do not have, but what I do have I give you: In the name of Jesus Christ of Nazareth, rise up and walk." And Peter took him by the right hand and lifted him up, and immediately the beggar's feet and anklebones received strength. We too have the Spirit of God in us to heal and transform us and those for whom we pray.

Please notice carefully that Jesus breathed on the disciples and said, "Receive the Holy Spirit." The Holy Spirit is the *power* in the believer to set the captives free. It begins in the heart of the believer and flows out to others. Every time we read and study the Scriptures, we are breathing in the life of the Holy Spirit. God is the Word, and the Word is God (John 1:1). "And the Word became flesh and dwelt among us" (v. 14).

> So Jesus said to them again, "Peace to you! As the Father
> has sent Me, I also send you." And when He had said this,
> He breathed on them, and said to them, "Receive the Holy
> Spirit. If you forgive the sins of any, they are forgiven them;
> if you retain the sins of any, they are retained."
>
> —JOHN 20:21–23

Scripture reading and declarations not only strengthen your spirit, but they also become life and healing as you breathe in the life of the Spirit.

The important key here in this subject of expecting and commanding the miraculous is to recognize the importance of the Holy Spirit and of specific, targeted, and anointed prayer. Everything must have its basis in prayer. It is a relationship with God and His Spirit established through prayer. It is a dependence on God alone. We never take credit for the miraculous event.

> Most assuredly, I say to you, he who believes in Me, the
> works that I do he will do also; and greater works than
> these he will do, because I go to My Father. And whatever
> you ask in My name, that I will do, that the Father may be
> glorified in the Son.
>
> —JOHN 14:12–13

The woman with the issue of blood had suffered for twelve years and spent all her money and substance trying to find healing. She didn't have an inheritance or a Spirit-filled grandma or mom praying for her, but one day with Jesus changed everything. Today is your day. God will utilize all your past experiences and issues, and just as Jesus healed this woman (Luke 8:43–47), healed the man possessed by a demon (Mark 5:1–20), and healed a man with a withered hand (Luke 6:6–11), the Lord Jesus will also heal anyone who dares to believe that He is still the healer today. When the enemy thought he had won, God restored them. Today God will also restore you.

THE POWER OF GOD WORKING IN US

The power of God *working in us* is the vital key that opens the door to the miraculous. It opens the door to enormous and unimaginable blessings. I didn't say this; God is saying this to us. Take a good look at this word, *working*. It means, "operational, functioning, acting, employed, succeeding, and at work." Action and obedience to God's Word will keep you on the cutting edge of the miraculous. Father God will do the impossible for us according to the things that are going on inside of our hearts and the things that occupy our minds. Our prayer life prepares us for all the assignments for the day. If you're not there yet, please read this book carefully and purpose and determine in your mind to wash yourself clean and allow God's healing power to invade and transform your life.

> Now to Him who is able to do exceedingly abundantly above all that we ask or think, according to the power that *works* in us.
>
> —EPHESIANS 3:20, EMPHASIS ADDED

God's Word is filled with examples of the power of God at work in the life of Jesus and of other believers.

+ Jesus was followed everywhere He went because of the signs, wonders, and miracles that followed His teachings (Matt. 4:23–25; 14:35–36; John 6:2, 26; 12:18).
+ Jesus revealed He was the Messiah through miracles (Matt. 11:4–6).
+ Miracles manifest the glory of Christ, the glory of God, the works of God (John 2:11; 9; 11:4).
+ God "confirmed" His word with signs and wonders following when the disciples preached and taught the word (Mark 16:20).

- Faith is required for miracles to take place. Jesus asked the blind men if they believed before He healed them (Matt. 9:28).
- Many people receive a miracle and never repent or live right. God's judgment is upon those who receive healings and miracles and do not acknowledge God or live for Him (Matt. 11:20–24; John 15:24).
- Miracles are also for unbelievers. Jesus healed the nobleman's son at a distance, and the man believed and his whole house got saved (John 4:48–53).

POWERFUL PRAYERS TO ACTIVATE MIRACLES

Prayer for wisdom and revelation

Father, You say, "Call to Me, and I will answer you, and show you great and mighty things, which you do not know" [Jer. 33:3].

I thank You, Father, for granting me the spirit of wisdom and revelation in the knowledge of Christ, to understand the deeper things of the Word of God [Eph. 1:17].

Prayer to overcome deception

Father, Your Word declares that by Your divine power You have given us everything we need to live a godly life. I thank You for empowering me to overcome all the deception of the enemy. Satan has no place in me in the name of Jesus [2 Pet. 1:3].

Father, Your Word declares that if I abide in You, and Your words abide in me, I can ask what I desire, and it shall be done for me. In the name of Jesus, I command all demonic interruption out of my life and the lives of my family members. Satan, take your hands off my territory, off my children, off my marriage, off my finances. I speak blessings of health and abundance into my life. No weapon formed against me shall prosper, and every tongue that rises up against me You shall condemn. Christ Jesus in me is my hope of glory. I cast fear, doubt, and unbelief out of my heart. Today I set into motion all of God's blessings and divine protection into my life and home. Thank You, my Father. In Jesus's name, amen [John 15:7; Isa. 54:17; Col. 1:27].

Declaration of faith

I recognize that my real enemy is Satan, and he is already a defeated foe. Thank You, Father, for the blood of Jesus has redeemed me from every curse and stronghold of the enemy. I take my position in Christ Jesus where no plan or strategy of Satan can enter to steal, kill, or destroy. I put on the whole armor of God, defeating every evil and foul spirit of hell. I have dominion over all the power of the enemy, and nothing shall hurt me. Thank You, Father, for this great promise. In the name of Jesus, amen [Col. 2:15; Eph. 1:22; Luke 10:19; Rev. 12:11; Heb. 4:2].

Prayer to receive power

Father, Your Word declares that I shall receive power when the Holy Spirit comes upon me. Fill me now with Your Holy Spirit and empower me to remain steadfast and free from all bondage. I align myself with Your Word and place myself in a position to be blessed by You. Thank You, Father, for this great promise. In Jesus's name, amen [Acts 1:8].

Prayer for financial prosperity

Jehovah Jireh, You are my provider. I thank You because You are the Lord my God who teaches me how to profit, and You lead me in the way I should go. Thank You for wisdom, for it causes those who love wisdom to inherit wealth. As I keep Your Word, You make me prosperous. Everything that I endeavor to do according to Your will, will prosper. Thank You for mercy and favor. Thank You for a steady income. Thank You for opening the doors of blessing and closing the doors of lack. Teach me how to become fruitful and how to invest wisely. Father, I will honor You with my tithes and offerings. Thank You, Father, for this great promise. In Jesus's name, amen [Isa. 48:17; Prov. 8:21; Josh. 1:8].

CHAPTER FIVE

PRAYERS AND SCRIPTURES TO WASH YOU CLEAN

*Wash yourselves, make yourselves clean. Put away the evil
of your doings from before My eyes. Cease to do evil. Learn
to do good. Seek justice. Rebuke the oppressor.*

—ISAIAH 1:16-17

YOU MUST UNDERSTAND that you cannot wash yourself clean by yourself. The Holy Spirit will help you. The scriptures and prayers in this chapter will also help you receive cleansing and forgiveness. You are not alone; even the angels are ready to help you. You must desire a real change. This book is about the miraculous. You must come to a place where you are fed up with the attacks of the enemy against you and your loved ones. If you're ready, your heavenly Father is also ready.

HOW CAN YOU WASH YOURSELF CLEAN?

First, you must desire a radical change and repent of all your known sins, habits, and characteristics that you know offend God and others. There must be a turning away from everything that is evil and causes you to be easily offended and angry. You must desire a profound transformation. If you constantly deal with impure thoughts and imaginations, if you have been deeply hurt, rejected, oppressed, abused, and wounded, these scriptures will help you receive restoration and God's peace. The end result should be a deep contentment and joy in your heart. Your family and friends will notice the changes. God's blessings will begin to flow in your life.

God is holy, and He desires honesty and sincerity from His children. As you apply the Word of God to your life—and by that I mean, as you develop faith in God and do everything in your power to become obedient, loving, kind, and teachable—you will start noticing immediate changes. Changes will include peace, self-control, and wisdom to make decisions, and good things will start happening to you. End each prayer by saying, "…in Jesus's name, amen."

PRAYERS AND SCRIPTURES FOR FORGIVENESS AND CLEANSING

Prayer for cleansing and forgiveness

> *Heavenly Father, please forgive me and cleanse me of all my sins and iniquities. Wash me and set me free from all the iniquities and sins of my parents and ancestors. I want to serve You with all my heart. I surrender my life to You.*
>
> Wash me thoroughly from my iniquity and cleanse me from my sin.
>
> —PSALM 51:2, NAS
>
> Purify me with hyssop, and I shall be clean; wash me, and I shall be whiter than snow.
>
> —PSALM 51:7, NAS

Prayer for cleansing and repentance

Repentance is necessary to receive God's blessings. This is something we must do—not something God does for us.

> *Heavenly Father, I repent of all disobedience and acts of rebellion against You. I realize that without You I am open to all of Satan's attacks. I turn my heart toward You and surrender my will to Your will. I plead the blood of Jesus over my life, and I thank You for washing me clean.*

Wash your heart from evil, O Jerusalem, that you may be
saved. How long will your wicked thoughts lodge within
you?

—JEREMIAH 4:14, NAS

Prayer to keep pure and bring thoughts captive

*Help me, dear Father, to keep myself pure and my heart from
evil. I take every thought captive to the obedience of Christ that
exalts itself above the knowledge of Christ and tries to control
my thinking. It will not dominate my life, in Jesus's name!*

Casting down arguments and every high thing that exalts
itself against the knowledge of God, bringing every thought
into captivity to the obedience of Christ.

—2 CORINTHIANS 10:5

This verse speaks to all believers. To stay clean, one must pay attention to the thoughts that invade the mind every day and learn to take
every thought captive to the obedience of Christ.

And now why are you waiting? Arise and be baptized, and
wash away your sins, calling on the name of the Lord.

—ACTS 22:16

Baptism is considered a washing away or burying of our sins, and a
resurrecting of a new life in Christ.

Prayer to be cleansed

*Father God, sanctify and wash me clean as I study and med-
itate on Your Word. Thank You, Holy Spirit, for bringing
understanding to my mind and a desire to obey and apply Your
Word to my life. Thank You for accepting me and transforming
my life to serve You and others.*

> Such were some of you. But you were washed, but you were sanctified, but you were justified in the name of the Lord Jesus and by the Spirit of our God.
>
> —1 Corinthians 6:11

Prayer for mercy and renewing of the mind

Thank You, Father God, for having mercy upon me and for washing me clean. Thank You, Holy Spirit, for renewing and regenerating my mind and teaching me how to understand and apply the living Word to my life.

But when the kindness and the love of God our Savior toward man appeared, not by works of righteousness which we have done, but according to His mercy He saved us, through the washing of regeneration and renewing of the Holy Spirit.

—Titus 3:4–5

Prayer to draw near to God and cleansing from an evil conscience

My heavenly Father, I draw near to You with a sincere heart. Cleanse me and wash me clean from all evil and anything in my conscience that can be a hindrance to my relationship and walk with You. Purify my heart with the blood of Jesus, and open my spiritual eyes to discern the wiles of the enemy. I love You, my Abba Father.

Let us draw near with a sincere heart in full assurance of faith, having our hearts sprinkled clean from an evil conscience and our bodies washed with pure water.

—Hebrews 10:22, nas

Prayer for cleansing in the blood of Jesus

Dear Abba Father, give me the strength every day to keep myself pure and free from all temptations. Help me to obey Your statutes and wise counsel, and to walk in Your freedom so that You may find me washed in the blood of the Lamb.

I said to him, "My lord, you know." And he said to me, "These are the ones who come out of the great tribulation, and they have washed their robes and made them white in the blood of the Lamb."

—REVELATION 7:14, NAS

Blessed are those who wash their robes, so that they may have the right to the tree of life, and may enter by the gates into the city.

—REVELATION 22:14, NAS

Prayer for cleansing and discernment

My Father, I want to be an example of Your love to my family and to others. I am willing and obedient. Open my spiritual eyes to discern the enemy's devices against my life. With Your help and the guidance of the Holy Spirit I will seek to help others and to be a light in the darkness. Cleanse me and wash me clean.

And his [Naaman's] servants came near and said to him, My father, if the prophet had bid you to do some great thing, would you not have done it? How much rather, then, when he says to you, Wash and be clean?

—2 KINGS 5:13, AMP

Wash yourselves, make yourselves clean; put away the evil of your doings from before My eyes! Cease to do evil, learn to do right! Seek justice, relieve the oppressed, and correct the oppressor. Defend the fatherless, plead for the widow.... If you are willing and obedient, you shall eat the good of the land.

—Isaiah 1:16–19, amp

Prayer for restoration and thanksgiving

Heavenly Father, I am so thankful that You have chosen me and are making me aware of Your great love for us. Thank You for the gift of righteousness and salvation, for cleansing me of all sin and iniquity. Thank You for pouring Your new life into me and restoring my relationship with You. Thank You for giving me a new life in Christ. I love You, my Lord and Savior.

It wasn't so long ago that we ourselves were stupid and stubborn, dupes of sin, ordered every which way by our glands, going around with a chip on our shoulder, hated and hating back. But when God, our kind and loving Savior God, stepped in, he saved us from all that. It was all his doing; we had nothing to do with it. He gave us a good bath, and we came out of it new people, washed inside and out by the Holy Spirit. Our Savior Jesus poured out new life so generously. God's gift has restored our relationship with him and given us back our lives. And there's more life to come—an eternity of life! You can count on this.

—Titus 3:3–7, The Message

Heavenly Father, help me to set my mind on things that are pure and not on things that feed my flesh. Thank You, Holy Spirit, for helping me walk in the light of God's Word (Rom. 8:5–7).

MY COUNSEL

Stop being a victim. If you have been hurt by someone and are still carrying the pain and hurt, it is time to put a stop to it. As long as you insist on dwelling and feeling the pain of abuse, hurt, divorce, trauma, negative words, an unkind parent, and so forth, you will never feel peace and victory in your life. You must release that thing—it is like a cancer that keeps eating away. Forgive the person or persons who hurt you. Release yourself and break the curse of bondage over your life. Set into motion God's blessings! Loose yourself free today! I was there years ago, but today I am free. It took a specific decision on my part. Once I said, "I forgive you, Dad," I was free. The chains came off. Stop feeling sorry for yourself and get over it! The best of your life is still ahead of you. Your children or your future children will inherit your freedom and not the curses of pain and abuse. Praise God!

CHAPTER SIX

THE GREATEST MIRACLE— OUR SALVATION

*Believe on the Lord Jesus Christ, and you will
be saved, you and your household.*

—ACTS 16:31

REGARDLESS OF WHAT you're facing right now, Jesus is the answer. The Holy Spirit is the one who reveals Jesus to us. Salvation is not just a prayer. It's not a specific system. *Salvation is a PERSON.*

Salvation has a compassionate and merciful heart. Salvation has attentive eyes, listening ears, desires, emotions, and nail holes in His hands and feet—it is Jesus. It is not just a prayer—but a person.

In Jerusalem we find a devout Christian named Simeon, who, at the prompting of the Holy Spirit, came into the temple, and when the parents brought the little child Jesus to him, he took Jesus up in his arms and praised and thanked God, saying, "For with my [own] eyes I have seen Your Salvation." (See Luke 2:25–30.)

WHAT DOES SALVATION HAVE TO DO WITH MIRACLES?

The LORD has made bare His holy arm in the eyes of all the nations; and all the ends of the earth shall see the salvation of our God.

—ISAIAH 52:10

I believe that many people think they are saved because one day they said the sinner's prayer, but in reality, nothing has changed for them. They are still doing the same things, having the same desires and temptations, and dealing with the same demons. They truly need a miracle.

Miracles are for every son and daughter of the kingdom of God, but there is a process that leads to the miraculous. A relationship and transformation has to take place—a turning around from the old ways to the new person we become in Christ. Father God will make all things new and meaningful when we accept His love and believe His Word.

We need an awareness and true understanding of who Jesus really is to be able to experience what it really means to be in the presence of God. It is this awareness that ushers us into the realm of the impossible where sickness, addictions, shackles, curses, depression, and broken children and marriages are made whole and restored by the presence and power of the Holy Spirit.

God has a purpose and unique design for each of us, but God cannot have fellowship with someone who has a sinful nature. Because the nature of man is sinful, a spiritual death has to take place where the sin nature dies and man is born again in Christ.

THE POWER OF THE BLOOD OF JESUS

> For this is My blood of the new covenant, which is shed for many for the remission of sins.
>
> —MATTHEW 26:28

It is only through the power of the blood covenant that reconciliation (payment, agreement) and restoration are made possible. Man receives the new nature of God when he makes a decision to "put on the new nature (the regenerate self) created in God's image" (Eph. 4:24, AMP). Christ Jesus already paid the price on the cross of Calvary.

Without the born-again experience, fellowship with God is not possible. In our own ability we cannot be saved or forgiven. It is only through the power of the Holy Spirit that change is possible. The first step is repentance (Acts 3:19–20).

Our Christ, the Messiah, is alive today. He wants to refresh us from the effects of the heat and the attacks of the enemy. Refreshing comes from the presence of the Lord.

Sin has always separated man from God. The blood covenant has given man a way out from eternal condemnation and an open invitation to eternal life by accepting Christ Jesus as Savior. This wonderful covenant is the answer to man's suffering and all kinds of abuse. The penalty of sin is death, but the reward of salvation is eternal life in the kingdom of God.

THE EFFECTS OF REPENTANCE

The decision to repent and to enter into a covenant relationship with God is a decision that each one of us can make as an individual. We cannot make the changes that are required—that is the work of God the Holy Spirit. As we choose to live in Christ, He makes the necessary changes in our lives that we are unable to make.

When we become equipped with the right knowledge and truth, we are able to walk in faith and enjoy the blessings and promises already designated and predestined for us. Immediately truth removes fear, doubt, and confusion, while at the same time the Spirit of God empowers us to live in freedom from the kingdom of darkness (John 8:31–32; 1 Pet. 2:9–10).

Our new clothes

When we accept Jesus Christ as our Lord and Savior, we are baptized into Christ and receive a new set of clothes. "For as many [of you] as were baptized into Christ [into a spiritual union and communion with Christ, the Anointed One, the Messiah] have put on (clothed yourselves with) Christ" (Gal. 3:27, AMP; see also 1 Cor. 15:53; Rom. 13:14; Rev. 3:5).

This new garment is Christ Jesus Himself, as He clothes us with

Himself when we accept Him as our Lord and Savior. As we enter into the provisions of the blood covenant with Christ, our heavenly Father sees us as He sees Jesus. We now have His victory, His wealth, and His rights. We become a new creation in Christ—forgiven and without our past (2 Cor. 5:17).

In the Book of Colossians we are also reminded of our high standard of living and renewal in Christ, a renewal in which there is no distinction of color or race and in which Christ is all and in all (Col. 3:10–12).

When we accept salvation, we are clothed with an eternal life insurance. We become new beings in right standing and holiness. We possess the nature of Christ, and we are clothed with His mercy, loving kindness, humility, and all His marvelous qualities.

Salvation guarantees new things.

> Therefore if any person is [ingrafted] in Christ (the Messiah) he is a new creation (a new creature altogether); the old [previous moral and spiritual condition] has passed away. Behold, the fresh and new has come!
> —2 CORINTHIANS 5:17, AMP

To become *engrafted* in Christ means, "to become attached, joined, fixed, embedded, implanted, spliced, married, merged, united and inserted." All these meanings are very significant and powerful. They denote possession, permanence, and ownership.

When a couple gets married, there are many obstacles to overcome. Each partner has to learn to know each other by listening, serving, being kind, merciful, and having lots of patience. For those who are teachable and allow God to be actively involved in their lives, many wonderful new things are in store for them.

Father God is the same way with us. He gives us lots of room and space to learn our new roles as children of God. Some learn fast, and some take forever to realize that wholeness and abundance are waiting in line to join with our new nature. My husband has a saying: "My pastor doesn't have a problem feeding a baby Christian a bottle, but he does have a problem when he has to separate his moustache to insert the bottle."

THE GROWTH PROCESS

Our supernatural life doesn't guarantee instant transformation or change. We don't become holy overnight. But we must accept that Jesus Christ has already paid the price for us to enjoy our salvation. Everything necessary for us to live a victorious and harmonious life has already been provided. God is waiting for us to take possession and appropriate all the awesome life-changing new things our salvation provides for us.

Growing, maturing, and developing our spiritual muscles will take time, patience, and much practice. Our Father knows this is a process of sanctification, but He wants you to understand that you now have a new position as an accepted member of the family of God. You're not an outsider looking in. You now have legal access to all of God's blessings. You also have the written Word of God to guide you and instruct you in all aspects of life and relationships. You have the power of the Holy Spirit resident in your spirit to guide your steps and teach you all truth.

For this great salvation to become your greatest joy and possession, you must nurture it and protect the relationship between you and the Holy Spirit. You must daily apply yourself to the discipline of conversing with Father God and listening and applying His wise counsel in the Bible. Spiritual food is necessary to survive the onslaught of the enemy. Without a daily dose of supernatural food, a Christian will become anemic and fruitless. A barren tree is no good to anyone. You cannot be effective without actively seeking the things of God.

GOD'S PERSONAL GIFTS TO YOU

No matter how messed up you were in your life of sin, salvation has provided you with the gifts of eternal life and a new identify in Christ Jesus.

> For by grace you have been saved through faith; and that
> not of yourselves; it is the gift of God.
>   —EPHESIANS 2:8

Our Father God has provided us with everything pertaining to life and godliness. There are so many blessings listed throughout the Holy Bible that it would take many books to define them. The gifts of eternal life, healing, deliverance from evil spirits, and the gift of restoration of our souls are just a few of the many miraculous gifts provided by God to His children (2 Pet. 1:2–7).

Many times doubt, fear, anxieties, tiredness, the news, and even familiarity can cause us to become lazy and distant from God. By allowing ourselves to drift and be tossed around by adversity, we open the door for the *little foxes* to creep into our lives. There has to be an absolute awareness of who God is and who we are in Christ Jesus. Without this certainty and knowledge, we tend to take our spiritual walk for granted. I believe this is one of the biggest reasons why so many Christians live in defeat and complain about their constant weaknesses. They become totally oblivious of the many gifts and blessings at their disposal. They become overwhelmed by the noise and clamorous voices in the world.

Not only has Father God provided us with many gifts and blessings, but He has also raised us up together with Him and made us to sit down together in the heavenly sphere (Rom. 8:29–30; Eph. 2:6). This is a spiritual position we hold in the spirit realm. We are spiritual beings just as Father God, Jesus, and the Holy Spirit are Spirit. As believers we rule and reign with Christ in heavenly places. Wow! A deeper understanding of this truth will open your heart to desire and receive all that God has for you in this life. Our battles must be fought in the spirit realm.

Salvation guarantees provision for healing.

Jesus paid the penalty for sin on the cross of Calvary so that we can be saved from eternal damnation. The blood covenant that took place when Jesus willingly gave His life as the ultimate sacrifice guarantees all of God's children redemption and forgiveness from all their sins and iniquities.

Healing from all sickness and disease is available to all believers the moment they receive salvation. Jesus was disfigured, mutilated, scourged, and brutally beaten as He hung on the cross, bearing our sins and iniquities. His appearance was so drastically changed that He became unrecognizable. His body was ripped apart and tortured.

The root of all sickness and disease is sin. Jesus took upon Himself every wracking pain, inflammation, wound, agony, despair, torture, scar, abuse, insult, mockery, despicable name-calling, taunting, and dreadful shame and wicked desire of His enemies. As a result, Jesus was disfigured more than any other human being.

> [For many the Servant of God became an object of horror; many were astonished at Him.] His face and His whole appearance were marred more than any man's, and His form beyond that of the sons of men.
>
> —Isaiah 52:14, AMP

Jesus was willing to pay the price for us. As a result, healing is the bread of all God's children. Many are sick because they do not know or understand this truth. At the end of this chapter there will be a prayer to receive healing. My husband and I will get into agreement with you on this prayer. When you believe in your heart and confess with your mouth that *you are healed by the stripes of Jesus*, the Spirit of God begins to manifest the healing in your body. I am living proof of this.

There is also an interesting instruction in the following scripture: "That we might die (cease to exist) to sin and live to righteousness" (1 Pet. 2:24, AMP). We can't skip this; it is too important and significant for Father God. Sin separates us from right standing. Sin separates us from the blessings and our healing. If there's known sin in your life, you can beg and pray all you want, and your healing will

not manifest. You must crucify that sin by confessing it and turning
away from it.

> He personally bore our sins in His [own] body on the tree
> [as on an altar and offered Himself on it], that we might
> die (cease to exist) to sin and live to righteousness. By His
> wounds you have been healed.
>
> —1 Peter 2:24, amp

Why Confess our Sins?

> If we [freely] admit that we have sinned and confess our
> sins, He is faithful and just (true to His own nature and
> promises) and will forgive our sins [dismiss our lawless-
> ness] and [continuously] cleanse us from all unrighteous-
> ness [everything not in conformity to His will in purpose,
> thought, and action].
>
> —1 John 1:9, amp

As you can see from this verse, when we admit and confess our sins,
forgiveness and cleansing take place in our lives. If people would
only understand the life-changing consequences of forgiveness and
cleansing from sin, they would be in line anxiously waiting to confess their sins.

Forgiveness means pardon, mercy, and compassion. Cleansing
means purification, washing, purging, decontamination, and refining.
It is not enough for a sinner to be forgiven. By cleansing, not only are
all the sins, contamination, and dirty habits forgiven, but also the
person is restored in his spirit, soul, and body. This is a *miracle* of restoration that only God can effectively produce in man.

What Is Sanctification?

Sanctification is cleansing. Cleansing is a process that detoxes a person
from sins and iniquities. The more cleansing we receive by applying

God's Word, the more the blessings from God will flow into our lives. Sanctification is also a process of beautification. The person becomes renewed as he or she commits and dedicates his or her life to serving God in Spirit and in truth. Cleansing also uncovers all the hidden treasure in us. You will notice a desire to excel and use your talents and abilities to please God and others.

Your body was created with an intricate and marvelous cleansing system that purifies your blood. In the spiritual realm the blood of Jesus cleanses you from all sins, iniquities, sickness, diseases, and pestilences.

How do we receive cleansing?

We receive cleansing by reading God's Word and applying the principles to our lives. For example, the Bible says in Psalm 34:13, "Keep your tongue from evil, and your lips from speaking deceit." We apply this counsel by learning and practicing to speak truth and encouraging words, rather than evil and negative words. The Holy Spirit is our helper and our teacher, and He is also the one who helps us understand the Bible.

OUR POSITION IN CHRIST

Our salvation and position in Christ are secure and irrefutable, for God cannot lie. Our relationship with Christ is sealed. He loosed and freed us from our sins by His own blood. He is our refuge, our fortress, and our protection (Rev. 1:5; Ps. 91).

Our salvation gives us entrance to all the benefits and wealth of the King of kings and the Lord of lords. We become a royal race of the kingdom of God Almighty. Praise God! (See Revelation 1:6.)

The moment we accept Jesus Christ as our Lord and Savior, we are accepting His life in exchange for our life. We are now in Christ, and all that belongs to Him also belongs to us. This spiritual exchange guarantees us all the benefits of Christ's resurrected life. As we consider ourselves dead to sin, we become alive to God in Christ Jesus.

Salvation is the beginning of an unbroken fellowship with Christ Jesus (Rom. 6:11).

As Marilyn Hickey says in one of her teachings:

> Christians with a poor self-image don't know their position in Christ. Our position is one of victory. Ephesians is the "sit, walk, and stand" book. Through Christ we sit in heavenly places, walk in victory and stand as conquerors.[1]

One of the things that I practice in my daily Christian walk is to announce and declare who I am in Christ Jesus. There is something unique and inspiring when you hear yourself declare a truth, especially about yourself. I declare my "position in Christ" when I'm taking a shower, driving, meditating, and even when I'm watching a movie or the news, or listening to music. Somehow it interjects in my mind, and I find myself unconsciously and consciously paying attention to something specific about my position in Christ. It has become such a habit that the scripture "I can do all things through Christ who gives me the strength" is the first thing that comes out of my mouth every morning. *Make this a habit, and the habit will become your identity!*

My identity and position in Christ

- I am a child of God and one with Christ (John 1:12).
- I am an overcomer in this world (1 John 4:4).
- The Word is medicine and health to all my body (Prov. 4:20–22).
- I am born of God, and the evil one cannot touch me (1 John 5:18)
- I am the salt of the earth (Matt. 5:13).
- I am the light of the world (Matt. 5:14).
- I am a new creation (2 Cor. 5:17).

+ I am united in Christ, and I am one spirit with Him (1 Cor. 6:17).
+ I am a partaker of the heavenly calling (Heb. 3:1).
+ I can do all things through Christ who gives me the strength (Phil. 4:13).
+ I am chosen by God to produce fruit (John 15:16).
+ I am an heir and joint-heir with Christ Jesus (Rom. 8:17).
+ I am an enemy of the devil (1 Pet. 5:8).
+ I am crucified with Christ, and sin does not have dominion over me (Rom. 6:1–6).
+ I have the mind of Christ (1 Cor. 2:16).
+ I am healed by the stripes of Jesus (1 Pet. 2:24).
+ I am prosperous as my soul prospers, and I walk in health (3 John 2).
+ No weapon formed against me shall prosper (Isa. 54:17).
+ I am a citizen of heaven (Eph. 2:6).
+ I am a member of the body of Christ (1 Cor. 12:27).
+ I am God's temple, and the Holy Spirit dwells in me (1 Cor. 3:16; 6:19).
+ My life is hidden in Christ (Col. 3:3).
+ I am justified by faith, and I have peace with God (Rom. 5:1).
+ The law of the Spirit of life in Christ has set me free from the law of sin and death (Rom. 8:2).
+ I am redeemed and forgiven through the blood of Jesus (Eph. 1:6–8).
+ I do not have a spirit of fear but of God's power (the Holy Spirit) and His love. I have a sound mind (2 Tim. 1:7).
+ I am complete in Christ (Col. 2:10).
+ I am blessed with every spiritual blessing (Eph. 1:3).
+ I am free forever from condemnation (Rom. 8:1).

- I am established, anointed, and sealed in Christ (2 Cor. 1:21–22).
- I have access to my heavenly Father through Christ Jesus (Eph. 2:18).
- I have access to the Father through faith in Him (Eph. 3:12).
- I have forgiveness of sins through the blood of Christ (Col. 1:14).
- All my needs are met according to His riches in glory (Phil. 4:19).[2]

Our identity

Our spiritual position and identity as joint-heirs with Christ Jesus are real and authentic. We hold a spiritual, supernatural, miraculous position and identity that qualify us to enjoy all of the benefits of the kingdom of God on the earth, as well as the kingdom of God in heaven. Our mark of authenticity is the Holy Spirit. We were sealed, marked, and branded as God's own possession. When we receive salvation, we receive a spiritual circumcision of the heart by the Holy Spirit, who puts His seal upon us as a guarantee. (See Ephesians 1:13–14; 4:30; Romans 2:28–29; 2 Corinthians 1:21–22; Romans 8:16.)

Make sure you read this entire chapter a few times. Our identity in Christ is powerful and effective when we have knowledge and understanding of all its benefits and conditions. Miracles will become an everyday event when we become sold out to the kingdom of God. Most of the time you won't even notice many of the miracles of protection and divine intervention from accidents, rip-offs, and the flying arrows from the enemy because they are supernatural. God's angelic warrior armies are constantly at work on our behalf, invisibly and visibly, ordering our steps, closing the mouth of the lions, and making sure that not one of our bones is broken. (See Psalms 91:5; 34:20.) Praise God!

The Importance of Reading God's Word

> Study and be eager and do your utmost to present yourself to God approved (tested by trial), a workman who has no cause to be ashamed, correctly analyzing and accurately dividing [rightly handling and skillfully teaching] the Word of Truth.
>
> —2 Timothy 2:15, amp

To understand and accept the written Word of God, it is absolutely necessary to study and read the Bible on a consistent and systematic basis. If we truly want to understand our new covenant relationship with Christ Jesus, we must make every effort to read and study the Bible. We must read not only to know our benefits and learn all about God's promises to us, but we must read the Word also because it produces cleansing every time we read it. The Word is the living water that purifies our soul, our thoughts, and our habits. "So that He might sanctify her, having cleansed her by the washing of water with the Word" (Eph. 5:26, amp).

- ✦ Reading the Bible produces God's life-transforming wisdom. God is the Word. God is all wisdom, knowledge, and understanding. "In Him are all the treasures of [divine] wisdom" (Col. 2:3, amp).
- ✦ Reading the Bible causes our faith to be developed and exercised (Rom. 10:14–17).
- ✦ Reading the Bible reveals the image of the Lord in us. The more we read, the more of His image we reflect (2 Cor. 3:15–18).
- ✦ Reading the Bible reveals to us our rights, responsibilities, and benefits of the blood covenant. Our relationship with the Lord becomes stronger and more intimate.

The more we read the Bible, the better witnesses we become and the more discernment we acquire to defeat the strongholds of the enemy. The Word of God is described as living water (John 4:10). It cleanses and purifies as it is applied to our spirit, soul, and body. We become agents of change and transformation in the lives of others as well as our own.

As we learn to read and understand the Word of God, the stronger and bolder our spirit man becomes. "No weapon formed against you shall prosper" (Isa. 54:17).

WE BECOME THE TEMPLE OF THE HOLY SPIRIT

Once saved, we become the *temple of the Holy Spirit*. The Holy Spirit of God now resides within us (1 Cor. 6:19–20). This is an awesome truth and responsibility. Everything we do, think, and say affects our relationship. We are not our own anymore. We must learn to bring glory to God in our body. This is God's covenant with us. A covenant is a legally binding agreement, contract, mutual promise, and pledge.

Father God wants our understanding and our heart to be flooded with light so that we can understand our calling and glorious inheritance in Christ. There is no limit to His power in us. It is immeasurable and surpassing greatness (Eph. 1:18–19).

My intention was to write a few paragraphs about the miracle of salvation in this chapter. But as I got deeper into the subject, I realized that not all Christians are aware of the precious gift of the Holy Spirit or the implications of such a great and awesome power in us. As I said in the beginning, salvation is a *Person*, not just a prayer of commitment. Christ has exchanged Himself for us in this covenant relationship by becoming the sacrifice and the gift. Our prayer invites the person of Jesus and the person of the Holy Spirit into our heart. Now that is powerful!

The moment we become sons and daughters, God sends His Holy Spirit into our hearts, crying, "Abba Father!" This is a supernatural miraculous event. (See Galatians 4:6; 1 John 3:24; 4:13; 5:6.)

Our obligation

It is not unusual that many Christians are not aware that their successes and open doors of blessing are the result of their covenant relationship and right standing with God. Many assume that it's their own intellect, hard work, and personal discipline. We must get our thinking aligned with truth and believe that God directs the steps of His *obedient* children (Ps. 37:23; Prov. 16:9).

It is our obligation and duty to stay connected every day with the Holy Spirit and to feed on the Word of God. There is no other source that can compare with the wisdom and power within its pages. If the Bible were the only book available to read in the whole world, we would probably be living in a world dominated by God's love, abundance, and peace.

> For the Word that God speaks is alive and full of power [making it active, operative, energizing, and effective]; it is sharper than any two-edged sword, penetrating to the dividing line of the breath of life (soul) and [the immortal] spirit, and of joints and marrow [of the deepest parts of our nature], exposing and sifting and analyzing and judging the very thoughts and purposes of the heart.
>
> —HEBREWS 4:12, AMP

I memorized this scripture years ago when I heard the testimony of a pastor friend who came to visit our home. He described how he had been diagnosed with cancer in his lungs, and his doctor told him that it would be a very delicate and expensive operation, without a guarantee that all the cancer could be arrested. As he shared his experience, his voice got louder and the excitement in his face was very evident. He confessed that he had no medical insurance and had no way of coming up with the large sum of money necessary.

On his knees one evening, he searched his heart and cried out for God's mercy. Three days later, after spending many hours in his private office, he opened up the Bible to Hebrew 4:12. This verse became *alive and full of power* to him. He lay flat on the floor, took his Bible, and placed it upon his chest, declaring, *"Father God, my Bible declares that Your Word is alive and full of power and that it is sharper than a two-edged sword, penetrating the dividing line of my soul and spirit, and of my joints and marrow and examining the thoughts and purposes of my heart. I now surrender to you and believe that Your Word is entering my joints and marrow and healing my lungs, eradicating cancer and effecting a miracle in my body, right now, in Jesus's name, amen!"*

Nothing happened immediately. He fell asleep on the floor, and when he awoke, he was breathing normally and without difficulty. He quickly examined himself, jumped up and down, and didn't feel the usual pain or shortness of breath. He effortlessly ran up and down a set of stairs and realized he was healed! Immediately he contacted his physician who, in total unbelief, diagnosed him free of cancer. I truly wish that I could document this miracle with a doctor's report and a signed document from this brother. But this was many years ago in my teen years, and I have no idea where this pastor is today. He was a friend of the family and a very honorable man. Only his family and close friends knew he had cancer. All I can say is that it left a lasting impression on my mind and spirit. I immediately memorized this scripture, and to this day, I lay my Bible on my chest and declare that I am healed. I've seen God's power set me free of many attacks of the enemy upon my life.

Your obligation and responsibility as a child of God is to trust God, believe His Word, and have faith that what He promises, He will do! We must learn to have absolute trust and confidence in His power, wisdom, and goodness. It is only by His Spirit that we have access to all the benefits of the blood covenant (Heb. 10:15–19).

The power of Satan is nullified when confronted by an obedient child of God. Satan recognizes the stamp and seal of the Holy Spirit upon a person. The sad part about all this is that many wonderful Christians do not understand all these truths. When Satan comes to shoot a fiery dart of doubt and unbelief, an uninformed Christian can be easily defeated by the enemy.

The Bible says, "My people are destroyed for lack of knowledge" (Hosea 4:6). Notice it says "My people"—God's people who accept salvation and trust God with all their hearts. It is your obligation and duty to attain knowledge and understanding of such a great salvation and of your covenant relationship. For God so greatly loved and dearly prized you that He gave His Son, Jesus, as a sacrifice to redeem you of your sins (Eph. 3:15–21; Phil. 4:13; John 3:16).

THE POWER OF THE HOLY SPIRIT IN US

> But you will receive power (ability, efficiency, and might) when the Holy Spirit has come upon you, and you shall be My witnesses in Jerusalem and all Judea and Samaria and to the ends (the very bounds) of the earth.
>
> —ACTS 1:8, AMP

Pay close attention to this verse, for it reveals a tremendously powerful truth. We are promised the power of the Holy Spirit to indwell us to be God's witnesses on earth and to have authority over all the power of the enemy.

What is the power of the Holy Spirit?

It is the same *power* that indwelt Jesus Christ as a man on the earth. The same *power* that healed the sick and worked miracles, cast out demons, and set the captives free. The same *power* that raised Christ Jesus from the dead. It is the same power that converted the water into wine and multiplied a boy's lunch to feed thousands. Praise God!

One of the greatest roles of the Holy Spirit is to teach us all things pertaining to the kingdom of God and the purpose for our existence. He directs a major part of our lives when we keep God's commandments. God empowers us through the baptism of the Holy Spirit to do His will and to live a victorious life.

The baptism in the Holy Spirit is the *power* (*dunamis*) of the Christian. It's the dynamite that ignites our soul with boldness to warfare in the spirit realm.

The tongues described on the Day of Pentecost are a language that the Holy Spirit understands. When we pray in the Spirit, we access God in a heavenly language. Satan does not understand this language. We don't understand this language, but the Holy Spirit does. It is the Spirit of God who prays through us when we need it the most. There are times when we pray and don't really know what the outcome of the situation we're praying about will be. But the Holy Spirit is wise, and as our helper and intercessor, He prays through us in a heavenly language. It is very comforting and reassuring. There's a peace that will take over the mind and spirit.

I love the way the Letter of Jude describes it in verse 20:

> But you, beloved, build yourselves up [founded] on your most holy faith [make progress, rise like an edifice higher and higher], praying in the Holy Spirit.
>
> —AMP

I was baptized in the Holy Spirit as a teenager and have never stopped praying in the Spirit. It has become a habit that I cherish, protect, and practice, especially when I need help in a situation that is beyond my control. There's a sense of peace when the situation is turned over to the Holy Spirit. My precious mother and grandmother prayed in the Spirit constantly. They saw many strongholds and evil plans of the enemy destroyed before their eyes.

There are many attributes of the Holy Spirit. Our knowledge of them will help us understand the tremendous role of the Holy Spirit in our lives. You can be assured that He is always waiting to help us. Some of the attributes of the Holy Spirit are listed here (AMP):

+ Teacher (Luke 12:12; 1 John 2:27)
+ Helper (John 15:26)
+ Guide (John 16:13)
+ Comforter (John 14:26; 15:26)
+ Counselor (John 14:26; 15:26)
+ Intercessor (John 14:26; 15:26)
+ Advocate (John 14:26; 15:26)
+ Strengthener (John 14:26; 15:26)
+ Standby (John 14:26; 15:26)

We must not neglect God's great gift of the Holy Spirit to us. God is involved in every aspect of our lives. If we neglect to nurture and protect this sacred relationship, the enemy will take advantage of us. Instead of living in absolute freedom and abundance, we will end up living in defeat and constant lack. The Holy Spirit is our helper and our teacher, and there is nothing too difficult for Him.

GOD'S EVERLASTING COVENANT

God's covenant with us is everlasting and absolute and cannot be violated (Ps. 89:34). It is up to us to enter into this covenant or reject it. It is only through the everlasting blood covenant that we have entrance to the throne of God. Forgiveness, healing, peace, provision, refuge, wisdom, knowledge, understanding, discernment, and everlasting life are just some of the benefits.

When a person truly understands the meaning of our glorious and magnificent inheritance in Christ, that person will never depart from serving and loving the true living God.

Demons do not flee because we shout out loud in the name of Jesus. They do not tremble because we wave our arms, scream, or speak in tongues. It is not our excitement that causes demons to flee, *but our relationship with Jesus Christ.*

> And the evil spirit answered and said, "Jesus I know, and
> Paul I know; but who are you?"
>
> —Acts 19:15

From the beginning of our covenant relationship, God established this promise: "It doesn't matter what the enemy tries to inflict upon you; I will protect you, and I will be your strength and your refuge. My right hand will deliver you and bear you up above your enemies."

Over and over we read in the Bible of God's promises to protect us from all harm and to encourage us to use our authority in the name of Jesus.

> The Lord is my strength and my shield;
> My heart trusted in Him, and I am helped;
> Therefore my heart greatly rejoices,
> And with my song I will praise Him.
> The Lord is their strength,
> And He is the saving refuge of His anointed.
> Save Your people,
> And bless Your inheritance;
> Shepherd them also,
> And bear them up forever.
>
> —Psalm 28:7–8

Prayers and Declarations

The apostle Peter said:

> Repent therefore and be converted, that your sins may be blotted out, so that times of refreshing may come from the presence of the Lord, and that He may send Jesus Christ, who was preached to you before.
>
> —Acts 3:19–20

Rededication prayer

> *Heavenly Father, I am making a quality decision this day to rededicate my life to You. I pledge my heart and my entire being and everything that I am to You. I sincerely draw near to You and thank You for accepting me and helping me to recover what the enemy has stolen. Please forgive me of all my sins and iniquities. Father, I now choose to forgive everyone who has sinned against me. I receive Your love and Your mercy. Thank you for guiding my steps and granting me a new beginning. Help me to change the things I can change and allow You to change the things I cannot. I surrender my life to you. I love You, my Lord and Savior. In Jesus's name, amen.*

Prayer to receive Jesus Christ as Lord and Savior

The Bible says that if you confess with your mouth, "Jesus is Lord," and believe in your heart that God raised Him from the dead, you will be saved. For it is with your heart that you believe and are justified, and it is with your mouth that you confess and are saved (Rom. 10:9–10).

To receive Jesus Christ as the Lord and Savior of your life, pray this salvation prayer with all your heart:

> *Lord Jesus, I desire to know You personally. Thank You for dying for me on the cross to redeem my sins. I open the door of my life and heart and receive You as my Lord and Savior. Thank You for forgiving all of my sins and giving me eternal life. Please take control of my life and help me to overcome. In Jesus's name, amen.*

Prayer to be filled with the Holy Spirit

Kenneth Copeland explains it this way:

> Your baptism in the Holy Spirit is received by faith. Jesus said in Luke 11:13, "If ye then, being evil, know how to give good gifts unto your children: how much more shall your

heavenly Father give the Holy Spirit to them that ask him?"
When you ask in faith, the Holy Spirit comes to live in
you. And when you are filled with the Holy Spirit, as in the
book of Acts, you speak in tongues....

The Holy Spirit was sent to be our Helper. So when you
pray in tongues, what actually happens is that the Holy Spirit
searches your heart and prays through you the perfect will of
God (Romans 8:26–27). You actually utter the secret truths
and hidden things that are not obvious to the understanding
of your mind (1 Corinthians 14:2, *The Amplified Bible*).[3]

If you really desire to receive the Holy Spirit as your helper into
your life, say this prayer and sincerely believe it in your heart:

"Heavenly Father, I am a believer. I am Your child and You
are my Father. Jesus is my Lord. I believe with all my heart
that Your Word is true. Your Word says if I will ask, I will
receive the Holy Spirit. So in the name of Jesus Christ, my
Lord, I am asking You to fill me to overflowing with Your
precious Holy Spirit. Jesus, baptize me in the Holy Spirit.

"Because of Your Word, I believe that I now receive and I
thank You for it. I believe the Holy Spirit is within me and,
by faith, I accept it. Now, Holy Spirit, rise up within me as
I praise God. I fully expect to speak with other tongues as
You give me the utterance."

Now begin giving sound to the expressions in your
heart. Speak and hear the Holy Spirit speaking through
you. Rejoice! You've just been baptized in the Holy Spirit!
You've been endued with power—hallelujah![4]

Prayer of commitment

*Lord, I give myself to You. Please accept every facet of my life,
and use me for Your honor and Your glory. I yield myself to
You right now. I desire to know You more intimately and to*

love You and obey Your Word. I am willing to do Your will and turn my back on all the things that rob my quality time with You. Today I affirm my love for You, my God. Thank You for wisdom, knowledge, and understanding. Today I commit to serve You with all my heart. In the name of Jesus, amen.

Prayer of agreement for a miracle

Father God, we stand in agreement with _____ [your name], believing Your Word, "...that if two of you agree on earth concerning anything that they ask, it will be done for them by My Father in heaven" [Matt. 18:19].

We believe Your Word will accomplish what we send it to do. We bind the works of the enemy and all manipulation and lying spirits; all sickness, disease, and family curses. We loose the spirit of truth and the power of Your Word to accomplish this miraculous healing.

In the name of the Father, the Son, and the Holy Spirit, we declare it done for Your glory, amen.

A LAST PRAYER

Father, I scarcely dare to pray,
So clear I see, now it is done,
That I have wasted half my day,
And left my work but just begun.
So clear I see that things I thought
Were right or harmless were a sin;
So clear I see that I have sought,
Unconscious, selfish aims to win.
So clear I see that I have hurt
The souls I might have helped to save,
That I have slothful been, inert,

Deaf to the calls Thy leaders gave.
In outskirts of Thy kingdom vast,
Father, the humblest spot give me;
Set me the lowliest task thou hast;
Let me, repentant, work for Thee![5]

—Helen Hunt Jackson

NOTES

1—THE MIRACLE OF SOUL TRANSFORMATION

1. Jacqueline Hurtado, "Superintendent: All of L.A. School's Teachers to Be Replaced," *CNN Justice*, February 6, 2012, http://tinyurl.com/brlnjmj (accessed June 5, 2012).

2. "Authorities: Powell Planned Deadly Fire for Some Time," Seattlepi.com, February 6, 2012, http://www.seattlepi.com/local/article/Blast-kills-husband-of-missing-Utah-woman-2-boys-3052040.php (accessed June 5, 2012).

3. Jennifer LeClaire, " Prophetic Word for 2012: Revival Begins With You," Charismamag.com, December 29, 2011, http://www.charismamag.com/index.php/blogs/the-plumb-line-by-jennifer-leclaire/32358-prophetic-word-for-2012-revival-begins-with-you (accessed June 5, 2012).

4. F. F. Bosworth, *Christ the Healer* (Grand Rapids, MI: Baker Publishing Group, 2008), 189.

2—THE MIRACLE OF DELIVERANCE FROM EVIL

1. "Santa Muerte," statistic cited on Wikipedia is sourced from Araujo Peña, Sandra Alejandro, Barbosa Ramírez Marisela, et al., "El culto a la Santa Muerte: un estudio descriptivo [The cult of Santa Muerte: A descriptive study]" (in Spanish), *Revista Psicologia* (Mexico City: Universidad de Londres), http://www.udlondres.com/revista_psicologia/articulos/stamuerte.htm (accessed June 6, 2012).

2. J. Lee Grady, "Whitney Houston and the Silent Shame of Addiction," Fire in My Bones, February 15, 2012, Charismamag.com, http://charismamag.com/index.php/fire-in-my-bones/32479-whitney-houston-and-the-silent-shame-of-addiction (accessed June 6, 2012).

3. Bill Johnson, "You've Got the Power!", *Charisma*, March 2012 http://www.charismamag.com/index.php/component/content/article/1622-features/32505-youve-got-the-power (accessed June 6, 2012).

4. Associated Press, "Alyssa Bustamante Verdict: 'Thrill Killer' Gets Life With Possible Parole For Killing 9-Year-Old Elizabeth Olten,"

Huff Post Crime, February 8, 2012, http://www.huffingtonpost
.com/2012/02/08/alyssa-bustamante-verdict_n_1262411.html
(accessed July 20, 2012). Permission to quote requested.

3—ACTIONS THAT PRODUCE MIRACLES AND HEALING

1. *Merriam-Webster's Collegiate Dictionary*, 11th ed. (Springfield, MA: Merriam-Webster, Inc., 2003), s.v. "miracle."

2. Daniel P. Sulmasy, "What Is a Miracle?", *Southern Medical Journal* 100, no. 12 (December 2007).

3. This section adapted from my testimony in *Satan, You Can't Have My Marriage* (Lake Mary, FL: Charisma House, 2010), 77–78.

4. Joan Hunter, *Healing for the Whole Man Handbook* (Springdale, PA: Whitaker House, 2006), 74–75.

6—THE GREATEST MIRACLE—OUR SALVATION

1. Marilyn Hickey, "Ephesians: Taking Your Position of Victory," Outline Notes by Marilyn Hickey Ministries, 1991.

2. Adapted from Iris Delgado, *Satan, You Can't Have My Children* (Lake Mary, FL: Charisma House, 2011), 131–134.

3. Kenneth Copeland, "How to Receive the Baptism in the Holy Spirit," Kenneth Copeland Ministries, http://www.kcm.org/real-help/article/how-receive-baptism-holy-spirit (accessed June 8, 2012).

4. Ibid.

5. Helen Hunt Jackson's last poem cited in Samuel M. Zwemer, *Taking Hold of God* (Grand Rapids, MI: Zondervan Publishing House, 1936).

EVERY HOME IS A TARGET

Filled with practical principles and Scripture-based prayers, these books by Iris Delgado provide you with the tools to stand with confidence and faith against Satan's attacks.

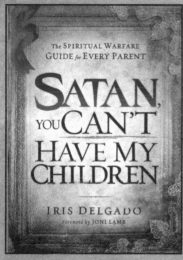

978-1-61638-369-5

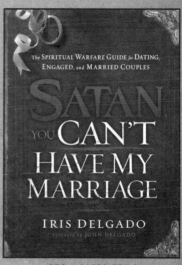

978-1-61638-673-3

FREE NEWSLETTERS
TO HELP EMPOWER YOUR LIFE

Why subscribe today?

- ❏ **DELIVERED DIRECTLY TO YOU.** All you have to do is open your inbox and read.

- ❏ **EXCLUSIVE CONTENT.** We cover the news overlooked by the mainstream press.

- ❏ **STAY CURRENT.** Find the latest court rulings, revivals, and cultural trends.

- ❏ **UPDATE OTHERS.** Easy to forward to friends and family with the click of your mouse.

CHOOSE THE E-NEWSLETTER THAT INTERESTS YOU MOST:

- • Christian news
- • Daily devotionals
- • Spiritual empowerment
- • And much, much more

SIGN UP AT: **http://freenewsletters.charismamag.com**

8178